If you want to walk on water, consider

STAYING IN THE BOAT

AND OTHER THINGS I WISH I'D KNOWN

JEFF LUCAS

CWR

To Kay
Thank you for 40 years of marriage, darling.
Looking back, there are many things I wish I'd known
about life, but one of the very greatest joys has been
knowing you.

Copyright © Jeff Lucas 2018
Published 2018 by CWR, Waverley Abbey House, Waverley Lane, Farnham, Surrey GU9 8EP, UK.
CWR is a Registered Charity – Number 294387 and a Limited Company registered in England – Registration Number 1990308.
The right of Jeff Lucas to be identified as the author of this work has been asserted by him in accordance with the Copyright, Designs and Patents Act 1988.
For a list of National Distributors, visit www.cwr.org.uk/distributors
Scripture references are taken from the Holy Bible, New International Version® Anglicised, NIV® Copyright © 1979, 1984, 2011 by Biblica, Inc.® Used by permission. All rights reserved worldwide. Concept development, editing, design and production by CWR.
Every effort has been made to ensure that this book contains the correct permissions and references, but if anything has been inadvertently overlooked the Publisher will be pleased to make the necessary arrangements at the first opportunity. Please contact the Publisher directly.
Cover image: Adobestock
Printed in the UK by Linney
ISBN: 978-1-78259-805-3

Once again, my thanks and appreciation to the team at CWR, and to the endlessly patient Lynette Brooks, who 'nudged' me gently into writing this book, and then acted like a Christian when I whined about my busy life.

And a special word of gratitude is due to Rebecca Berry, editor of this little tome. Her editorial skill, woven with gracious kindness, made the journey from first draft to published book an easy stroll rather than an irksome hike. Thanks, Rebecca.

My thanks also to the editorial team at Premier Christianity *magazine, which is where some of these thoughts first saw the light of day.*

Finally, my endless appreciation should be expressed to Kay, who has stayed at my side when I didn't know what I know now. And she's there still, when I still don't yet know what would be useful to know…

I'm very, very grateful.

Contents

Introduction

When I became a Christian 44 years ago, I was ecstatic... briefly. Perhaps 'giddy' would be a better word. When you're spinning in giddy delight, you laugh out loud with the thrill, but then feel disorientated. You're unstable on your feet for a while. That was me. (Come to think of it, that's still me.)

Relieved to be forgiven for my teenage sins and enthralled to be part of a warm, loving church community that literally opened its arms to me, I was very glad to be home. But my joy was matched by anxiety, an agitation that grew alarmingly. Home I was, but it was a new home, and I didn't know how to find anything. I felt the panic of a person who has invited some friends over for a delicious home-cooked meal, but is throwing every kitchen cupboard door open in frantic search of a frying pan even as the grinning guests arrive.

Suddenly I was surrounded by people who were utterly passionate about their faith. They didn't just have a mild dash of religion, vague faith that appeared on Sundays and made a temporary token appearance at Christmas and Easter. No, these people were very committed to their cause and their God. For them, Christianity was no add-on or addendum – it sat squarely at the centre of their lives. They talked animatedly about a God who was busily at work in their everyday humdrum: it was He who provided that parking space out of nowhere, He who managed to get some cash to them just when they needed it, and He who spoke to them quite a lot. With some of them, God seemed very talkative indeed. I listened hard for a voice, but apparently the line was down, or so it seemed at times.

Enthralled, I wanted to be like them, and I wanted my experience to mirror theirs. I coveted their confidence; their certainty; what seemed to be their crystal-clear hotline to God. I envisaged that one day I would pass through a spiritual sound barrier and, with an accompanying and reassuring sonic boom, I would suddenly understand. I would know God more, find prayer easier, and be impervious to my youthful temptations. But in the meantime, I felt like a man in a clapped-out Robin Reliant trundling around at a Ferrari convention. Their faith purred and motored forward in sleek style; mine spluttered and coughed and juddered, and it felt like the gearbox was about to give up the ghost.

Desperate to know more about the Bible, my own ignorance frustrated me. Back then most people in my church circle used the King James translation of the Bible, which was very useful in 1611, but occasionally incomprehensible in 1973. A few had The Living Bible, but some viewed it rather sniffily with suspicion. Someone told me it was not a translation, but a 'broad interpretation'. Nervous that I might be compromising if I read biblical truth in language that wasn't nearly 400 years old, I continued my daily wrestling with the King James' endless *thees*, *thous* and *yea verilys*. I felt good because I was reading the Bible, and bad because I couldn't make much sense of what I was reading. Yea verily, great was my confusion therein, and concerning most of what I mused over, I did wist not. You getteth my drift.

My lack of understanding was bewildering, and I felt lost. Although I was in church just about every time the doors were open (I drew the line at the ladies' meeting because they were all very old and – rather obviously – ladies), I wasn't miraculously downloading wisdom. I was, however, blessed with one of the most loving, caring pastors. Brian Richardson was a local minister who had found Jesus as a result of looking into a ditch. I'm not sure what was secreted down there in the murk, but the former atheist immediately became a believer, and then a church leader. A man with a smile that took over his whole face (and a heart to match), Brian listened to my angst-fuelled questions with patient grace. Brian laughed a lot, but he never laughed at the inane insecurities of a new believer like me.

There was so much I had to learn, and I didn't know then that true learning is not just about completing a course, following a manual, or reciting, parrot-style, a series of memorised facts. In real learning, life itself, with all of its ups and downs, is the classroom. Our everyday is the academy. Wisdom takes time to develop – a lifetime. What matters is that we learn from our wrong turns and mistakes, and continue to grow. I wish I'd known that maturity takes a while.

Over four decades later, all my questions have *not* been answered, and perhaps some never will be. (I'm nervous around those people who say that they'll get all the answers in heaven, as if they're planning on approaching the Lord and saying, 'Excuse me, Jesus, I know ten billion angels are singing right now, but could I just ask you about how to correctly interpret the book of Revelation?') And, actually, I'm fine with not knowing all the answers because one truth that I have figured out is this: I'm not God, and He alone knows.

But as I've trekked the trail called life, I have picked up a few nuggets along the way (I'm taking a risk – you might think that what I call a gold nugget of wisdom is more of a dull briquette of common sense). Nevertheless, I'd like to pass some of these nuggets/briquettes along in this book.

A clarifying word about the title, if I may: some readers might be aware that there is something familiar about it, and you're right. Some years ago the brilliant John Ortberg penned an enjoyable, inspirational bestseller called, *If You Want to Walk on Water,*

You've Got to Get Out of the Boat. The book has helped millions, and I want to make this absolutely clear: 'Staying in the Boat' is in no way a rebuttal or response to anything Mr Ortberg has to say. But in listing one of the things I wish I'd known, I simply identify this fact: Peter walked on water; his disciple friends stayed in the boat. Peter stepped out on the turbulent waves because Jesus summoned him; the others were not invited to participate, and they were probably glad to be so omitted. Not all of us are called to the same exploits; knowing our limitations is vital. More of that later, but for now let me say that Ortberg rightly calls us to be faithful when God is expanding our horizons; I'm calling us to faithfulness when we nudge up against immovable constraints. For a balanced view, buy John's book as well as this!

Thanks for joining me, and I hope you'll find my discoveries helpful, and even enjoyable to read as well.

C'mon. Let's continue the trek. Onward and, hopefully, upward.

Jeff Lucas
Colorado, 2018

I wish I'd known...
THAT ENCOURAGEMENT BRINGS STRENGTH

I love Facebook. I hate Facebook. I vacillate between the two.

I read a moving, real-life story of courage or faith, and I'm inspired. Real-life stories do that.

But then I ponder the photographs that some people post, capturing images of (a) this morning's breakfast – what a beautiful slice of bacon that was; (b) their new fluorescent lime green socks; or (c) the nasty bruise they got on their left calf while playing hockey yesterday... and I feel indifferent.

Worse still, I scan the accumulated rants of some Christians who are engaged in a furious row over some minor apostrophe in Leviticus. My eyes run over the CAPITAL LETTERS and the exclamation marks (!!!!!!!!) and I feel soul-sinking despair. It must be tiresome being right all the time, as these bellowing, blustering believers are. It's exhausting reading their smug homilies.

But it's even more debilitating when I'm personally on the receiving end of an online jolly-good-telling-off. Some years ago, while I was in Minehead speaking at a Christian conference (it happens at springtime, when they bring in the harvest), I 'enjoyed' being awakened every morning by screaming seagulls. They began their squawking serenade at 5am. I made the mistake of posting this tongue-in-cheek Facebook update: *Jeff would like to leave a little something for the noisy seagulls. Like a hand grenade.* Within minutes, my Facebook page was alive with tut-tutting messages from irate Christians who wanted me to know that Jesus loves seagulls as much as He loves me (an interesting thought that I don't have time to discuss here, but I wonder if He also has the same level of love for the chicken that graced my lunch today). I got a mass rebuking for what was intended as a mildly humorous comment.

Media makes anyone who does anything publicly an easy target. Just this week I got a sarcastic email from someone because they thought I was mocking a plummy accent during one of my radio broadcasts. They accused me of being racist, said I should be more kind and accepting, and then informed me that they'd never listen to or read my stuff again (which didn't seem terribly kind or accepting). I can therefore safely mention the incident here with little risk of offending them further.

Some years ago, one of my Facebook posts created an even greater stir than that – another throwaway comment that created mass confusion. I mentioned in one post that I was planning to change my name.

People were bewildered, understandably. Was this chap formerly known as Jeff following in the footsteps of the artist formerly known as Prince? What on earth was I doing? The answer was simple: I was changing my name to 'Grandad'. Within days, Stanley Benjamin was born and made my world a far brighter place.

But my little ruse got me thinking. In biblical history, the changing of someone's name was usually loaded with significance. Abram became Abraham, the father of nations. Jesus gave a tempestuous fisherman called Simon a name change, and he became Peter, the Rock. Saul, vicious persecutor of Christians, became apostolic preacher Paul. And in the early days of the infant Church, a chap formally known as Joseph was dubbed Barnabas (which means 'son of encouragement') and he lived up to his name.

It was this Joseph/Barnabas name change that really caught my attention, because I'd like a name just like his. How amazing to be named after a primary trait like encouragement. If I was named after my primary physical trait, I'd probably be dubbed something like 'Lucas-who-has-a-nose-that-can-see-round-corners'. I'm equally humbled and challenged by the thought of ever being named after my primary personality trait. Joseph/Barnabas must have been encouraged himself by being named a son of encouragement.

But being an encourager is surely not just a matter of temperament or disposition, even though there are some who seem more naturally inclined to cheer others on. For most of us, encouragement comes from discipline – we can *choose* to cheer. It's too easy to drift into cynicism, or even march around as a stern critic. How swiftly we can become picky, awkward, hard-to-please people, rarely carrying a smile. But encouragement costs nothing to give, and it does more than anything money can buy! A word of sincere encouragement (insincere encouragement given for false motives is called flattery, and totally devalues the currency of encouragement) can send the clouds packing, and energise the weary with the strength to walk another mile.

I've experienced that personally.

I am so grateful that, as I travel in ministry, so many people are incredibly kind and encouraging to me. It's always a delight to hear that a sermon or a book has been helpful to someone on their journey. Some people preface their gracious words of encouragement by saying, 'You probably hear this all the time, but I just wanted to say thank you.' Truthfully, it never stops being helpful to know that in some small way, someone's life has been impacted. Recently, a lady took my breath away with her words of appreciation: 'You matter to a lot of people, Jeff. You're very precious to us. We feel like you're on our side.' I know I risk sounding pretentious in sharing her comment here, but I was deeply moved by her carefully chosen words. She let me know that it was not just my ministry that mattered to her, but my life meant something, and she told me *why* it meant something.

And encouragement is especially welcome in the darker seasons of life. Forgive the personal disclosure, but the past couple of years have been wintry for me. My mother finally succumbed to dementia, and I had the honour and challenge of leading her memorial service. In a short space of time, Kay and I lost a number of dear friends – three in tragic accidents, two to long-term illnesses. Emotionally, I have felt exhausted and hopeless at times. This is where I am supposed to say that through it all, God has felt close and has strengthened me for the journey. That's not true. If anything, I have felt alone and, at times, abandoned. Perhaps you know the feeling. If my words seem shocking, the psalmist certainly experienced the desolation of feeling that God had relocated somewhere far, far away, and hadn't bothered to leave a forwarding address.

And then our world seems to be overdosing on bad news. Terrifying hurricanes devastate entire islands in the Caribbean. A rage-filled gunman spends ten carnage-creating minutes spraying bullets at a helpless crowd of country music lovers, just out for a night of fun. A church becomes a killing zone in Sutherland Springs, Texas. And then a man with a terrible haircut in North Korea exchanges playground insults with a man with a terrible haircut in the White House, and suddenly we're talking about the possibility of nuclear war. It all feels overwhelming.

After another sleepless night of crying out to God for some evidence of His ongoing care in a world of such random pain, an email arrived filled with kind encouragement, quoting a verse that has been a lifeline for me: 'my grace is sufficient for you'. We could read this as, 'I am with you – that is all you need'. This is the statement that God uses so often when His people are struggling. He doesn't promise a carefree life, without struggle or doubt. And to be honest, His comfort often comes more as a hint or a whisper rather than a shout. But faith says that we are not alone, and that we shall never, ever be alone again. We are not destined to trek through life unaccompanied. Whatever we feel (or don't feel), faith declares this: God is with us.

But more often than not, the comfort of God comes through people. We're not called to stand on our own two feet. The common suggestion is that true strength is proved when we live self-sufficient, independent lives, because we can't count on anyone but ourselves. But this is a false and foolish notion, as the life – and death – of Jesus shows.

I recently stood in the Garden of Gethsemane with a group of friends that were part of a tour to the Holy Land. The tortured look of the trees fittingly portrayed all that happened there, as Jesus spent an agonising evening there in the hours before His arrest, trial and execution. He knew what was coming, and willingly submitted Himself to it. But despite the fact that God's plan of human redemption was being played out, Jesus felt terrible anguish in that garden – and so He specifically sought the warmth and encouragement of human friendship, wanting His friends to not only be with Him in His wrestling, but to be praying with Him too. Jesus needed strength from the Father. And He needed the companionship of His closest friends and inner circle: Peter, James and John. Of the Twelve, those three alone had been privy to some of His most glorious moments and His darkest times too.

So who is there in your orbit that could use a phone call, a handwritten note, or a kind word from you today? With a random act of kindness, go ahead – make someone's day. Your words might transform a wintry, dreary morning into an unexpected springtime.

And it's not just about the words we *say*; we can encourage by receiving the words of others (in short, by listening). One casualty of the hypermedia age is the simple art of truly hearing others. Most conversations are dialogues of the deaf – exchanges between those who are perfectly able to hear audibly, but just don't listen. An attentive listener is rare. When we listen, we make a profound statement with our pause and silence. We communicate that others matter, and that their opinion counts. When we listen, we demonstrate patience, showing that we are willing to travel with others in their thought processes as they think out loud. And by listening I make a statement about myself: that my own voice is not the sweetest sound to my ears. Jesus spent so much time listening, and not just talking. The one who really did have so much to say made space for others to talk.

Sometimes we say it best when we say nothing at all – and just listen. And when we speak kindly, and listen attentively, we become just a little bit like God. When I give authentic encouragement, I become Christlike, because God is an amazing encourager.

As I write, our dear, long-term friends and colleagues in ministry, Paul and Priscilla Reid, are staying in our home. Paul just shared how one of their grandchildren reported that God had spoken to him when he was out in the garden. Playing on the trampoline, he said, 'I just heard from God for the first time.'

His parents were intrigued, and asked him what God had said.

'Well, I was singing some songs to God, and suddenly, as I was jumping up and down, God just said, "Bravo!"'

Perhaps you're tempted to dismiss this as childhood fantasy. But let's remember that we love and serve a God of grace and encouragement, the one who cheers us on, even in the most mundane activities and acts of service. This is the God who tears the heavens apart to affirm His Son as His baptism takes place; this is the God who runs with us and yet cheers us on as we run the race; this is the God who wants us to know that He is interested in the smallest details of life, including, it seems, bouncing on the trampoline. God is not the one who despises our acts of service, squashes our dreams and scoffs at our sacrifices: rather, He will say, 'Well done!', or 'Bravo!'.

So, in faith and faithfulness, know the 'bravo' of God. And pass a bravo on to someone else today.

Go ahead. You know it makes sense. As for me, I'm off to encourage a seagull.

Just kidding. Don't write in.

I wish I'd known...
THAT IT'S OK NOT TO HAVE A DEATH WISH

I don't have a death wish. When it comes to upcoming events that I'm looking forward to, 'stop breathing' is not on my list.

There you are. I've got that off my chest, and please don't judge me for it. But I've met some Christians who are apparently thrilled about their own future funeral, even though they won't care what's in the sandwiches they serve afterwards. Recently, I've been hearing believers talk a lot about the notion that we should all come to a place of 'maturity' in our Christian lives where we would rather die and be with Jesus than live here on earth. They give the impression that death is something to be warmly welcomed, a wonderful carrier that will usher us into the presence of the Lord, which is far better than the struggles of life here. But surely we are not called to see life like that. Yes, life is transient; it comes and goes so quickly. Nevertheless, this life is not just a holding room for eternity.

Odd though all this 'death wish' thinking seems at first glance, it's not hard to see where the belief comes from. The faithful apostle Paul was able to say that he longed to depart and be with Christ, which is far better. For him, to live was Christ, to die was gain. Life – nil points, death and eternity thereafter – ten points. Death scored much higher.

I'm glad that Paul reached that place of peace in the face of his upcoming demise. But I'm not there yet, and for the next couple of decades at least, I hope I don't arrive at that destination of happy resignation. I don't view death with the delirious delight of a five-year-old about to board an aeroplane for the first time. I think that when it comes to expiry, I'll be kicking and protesting and wanting to eek out every last breath. I remember the sinking feeling when, as a child riding a fairground ride, I saw the attendant place his hand on the lever that meant my fun was almost over. That's how I feel about life. Sir, kindly step away from that lever, if you please.

As for rather-keen-on-dying Paul, consider the context of his remarks. Over an extended period, Paul had experienced terrible pain and persecution as a follower of Jesus, as well as a series of unjust, kangaroo court trials that were corrupt to the core. Even though he enjoyed a measure of freedom at the end of his life, he was still under house arrest in Rome, and life was certainly not what it had been. He was no longer able to embark on missionary travels. The churches that he'd founded were beyond the horizon now. He couldn't visit them anymore, and surely fretted about the believers that he'd apprenticed. And so perhaps the exhaustion and frustration of it all made the glory of eternity shine all the brighter for the brave apostle. Being with Christ would be a welcome relief under those circumstances. Little wonder he anticipated it with such joy.

But that's not my experience, and so I have no desire to die just yet. Surely life is a beautiful gift, so precious that when God wanted to show the extent of His boundless love for us, His Son paid the ultimate price, in the giving up of His life at the tender age of 33. Surely we are designed and made to want to hold on to life for as long as we can. The resilience of the human body testifies to that truth. I've watched as impossibly fragile seniors – little more than skin and bones, their bodies riddled with cancer – fight on for weeks and months, clinging with vice-like tenacity to the gift of living. Death, while it is a defeated enemy, is still an enemy.

I've even heard that we believers should not experience sorrow when someone that we love passes away, which I think is total tosh. 'They're with Jesus, and so you should be glad about that,' some murmur piously. But that's just the point. The fact that he or she is there with Him means that he or she is not here with me.

'Some Christians try and comfort the bereaved with statements like, "It's like they're just in the next room",' my friend Adrian Plass laments, adding ruefully, 'But they're not. I've checked.'

When someone we love dies, we should grieve. Death still strikes a death blow, and tries to convince us that the cold abruptness of the grave is truly final. Resurrection hope can seem tenuous when someone we dearly love passes. But we grieve with hope, and hold on to the belief that life goes on beyond the grave. A brighter day is coming. But, that said, it's not death that's a sweetheart, but rather the truth of the resurrection that brings us that hope. Let's remember that when we are trying to comfort those who grieve. Jesus wrestled, not only with the painfulness of death to come, but with the parting He experienced from His friends, His disciples. And so while death should not intimidate us, I don't think we should feel guilty if we don't relish it.

And then there's a right way to respond when someone we love is given a terminal diagnosis. Yes, we pray, and encourage the person with the knowledge that God is mighty, and is able to heal. But in some cases, fervent prayer can push people into denial. They refuse to accept that there might be any other outcome than healing. Acknowledging that the suffering person might actually die is seen as lack of faith, even though the statistics concerning the certainty of death are rather impressive. Even up to the last minute of the terminally-ill person's life, some still insist on declaring healing. I've actually heard of Christians who, refusing to accept that the much-prayed-for person has died, have spent time trying to raise them to life again.

I know – Jesus did that to the rather smelly Lazarus. But while it might still happen occasionally, it's not the usual way. And if we deny that death is coming, there's the risk that people die without having the opportunity to say goodbye to family and friends. It's not that they were taken suddenly, in an accident that robbed them of any farewell; rather, it was bad theology that cancelled the possibility of any loving words being shared as they lingered on their deathbed. Worse, if the patient knows that their demise is very near, they can die with a sense of lingering shame, because they didn't have quite enough faith to get the 'result' that they so longed for – or so they fear. But faith is not about denial, but affirmation – affirming that Jesus is stronger than sickness, and if death comes, He has robbed even the grave of its power. And so we pray for the best, but prepare for the worst, knowing that the worst is painful, but temporary.

Surely a simple example of this can be found in the way that Jesus prepared for His own death. At the last supper, He bid His friends goodbye in a poignant covenant meal. There will be wine shared again, He promised, but it will be the vintage reserved for the fullness of the Father's kingdom. There's a parting. He carefully prepared for the worst – the cross.

But then a little later, in the shadows of Gethsemane, He asked the Father if there was any other way for the great rescue to be accomplished. He expressed His hopes for the best. They were denied, for He had to drink that cup of suffering to the full, but He asked repeatedly anyway. Ask for the best. Prepare for the worst.

So when death finally makes an appearance in my life, I want to be able to face it down with courage, and to gather my family and friends and say goodbye. But in the meantime, I want to live to the full, for and with Christ – today, and hopefully tomorrow, and for many days more too.

Death, kindly take your hand off that lever, right now.

I wish I'd known...
THAT BEING SEEN MATTERS

It's an old adage, apparently dating from the fifteenth century, and one I've never liked: children should be seen and not heard. It's a nasty notion: let's enjoy the pleasant sight of children to warm our hearts, but be impervious to the untimely demands that their interruptions might create.

The truth is, whether we are children or adults, we all want to be seen. Today, one of my grandsons performed a spectacular kick – a perfect volley of a football. The moment after he did it, he immediately turned around to see if he had been seen. 'Look, Grandad! Did you see that?!' What he really meant was, 'Did you see me doing that?'

Growing up, I experienced the opposite. I felt *heard* by my parents – they cared for me, provided and protected – but I didn't feel very *seen*, or noticed in my home. It's not that my parents were bad or consciously neglectful. But like swimmers hampered by leaden boots, frantically treading water just to stay afloat, they were preoccupied with survival and trying to hold a home together. They married shortly after the end of the Second World War. My father had languished for five long years behind barbed wire, his youth stolen as a prisoner of war, until at last he'd escaped. His innocence hijacked by half a decade of incarceration and near starvation, who knows what inner gremlins he wrestled?

My mother carried her own scars. Abandoned by her father in infancy (one day he just walked out of the house and never returned), she too was a wounded soul – plagued by depression before depression really had a name. Her stepfather embraced the 'children should be seen and not heard' philosophy; I was terrified of him.

Expected to get out and get a job to contribute to the family income as soon as possible, education was denied my mum. She left school at 14 and was placed 'in service' as a housemaid in a palatial home. Forget the romantic portrayal of the downstairs community in Downton Abbey; every day she watched a privileged few enjoy a life of luxury that was as foreign and unreachable to her as a distant planet. Her confidence was dented, irreparable: she never learned to drive, failing test after test until at last she gave up.

Money was short in our home; Dad worked long hours as a maintenance engineer just to keep the family afloat. And my mother did a marvellous job caring for my grandfather, who lived with us. A bowel cancer survivor, his colostomy meant that putrid dressings had to be changed throughout every day, a task that fell to my mum. My parents did unbelievably well just staying together under such pressures.

I share all this not to create some 'when I was a lad, we had to walk 20 miles barefoot in the snow to get to school' picture, but because I'd be remiss if I didn't mention the very real challenges my parents endured. And surely because of it all, I felt rather unnoticed. I know this not as a result of much psychotherapy, but because I remember one very exciting day in our family's life; one that embarrassingly shows how starved I was of attention.

I think it happened when I was about 12 years old. Our house was burgled while I was alone there. Nothing was taken, but drawers were left flung open and stuff scattered everywhere as the robber searched in vain for something valuable to plunder. The police were called, and I gave a statement. As it turned out, the thief did get away with something valuable that day, because the thief was me. I staged a break-in just to get noticed, and it worked. I think the kindly policeman knew it was me.

Unmotivated, my scholastic achievements were lacklustre at best. University was never a subject broached, and so I assumed that I would follow my father, uncles and brother into the company that they all worked for: I would service lifts and escalators. Thankfully, this never came about. (The result would have been vast numbers of people stranded on the ground floor, or stuck between the third and fourth. I have zero skill in anything practical or mechanical. A major triumph for me is the correct wiring of a 13-amp plug. Any attempts that I have ever made in the DIY department have prompted my family to gather for a time of intercessory screaming.)

Unimpressed with my careless attitude, my schoolteachers were largely indifferent – that is, until I joined Mr Ruff's class. An avid cricket fan and lover of Sussex real ale, Mr Ruff taught English, and quickly decided that it was a subject that I could possibly do well in. This was very good news, because I was mediocre at everything else. I disliked chemistry, mainly because the teacher in charge had almost blown his head off in an experiment that went wrong, which didn't inspire much confidence. History was dull, I hated my art teacher (the feeling was mutual), and I was so bad at maths that I didn't even bother to show up for my GCSE exam. I still cannot perform basic multiplication or division sums to this day.

But English – that was another story (literally). Mr Ruff told me that I was pretty good at stringing sentences together. More than that, he looked into a crowded classroom filled with adolescents who were aghast at the idea that Shakespeare was interesting, and saw me. Like a moth to light, I responded to his interest, and gained a double 'A' at A-level. Being seen was the key that unlocked my potential. All these years later, I've tried in vain to track Mr Ruff down so that I could treat him to a pint of best bitter, and maybe a steak to go with it. He saw me, and it changed my life. And there was another teacher, Mrs Richardson, who taught Religious Education. I had no interest in the subject, but felt drawn to her, because she showed caring interest in me. I didn't know then that her husband, Brian, would become my pastor, and do a wonderful job at it too. These people saw me. I loved them.

One of my favourite Bible stories is the one about Zacchaeus, not least because it always makes me imagine Danny DeVito parked up in the branches. In a sense, Jesus was a dead man walking, passing through Jericho on His way to Jerusalem, fully aware of what would befall Him there. But despite this, He was not walking with a head-down, furrowed-brow, I'm-on-the-way-to-save-the-planet attitude. Wonderfully, He saw the diminutive swindler, which was a big surprise in itself – but one greater was to follow, as Jesus invited Himself over to the taxman's home for lunch. Probably prompted only by the joy of being noticed, at the banquet that followed, Zaccheaus announced his sudden retirement from swindling, and determined to make massive reparations.

The Jewish theologian Martin Buber speaks of the distinction in our minds between treating people as subjects or objects. By objects, he means the propensity in our world for us to see others for what use they might have for us, or reducing them to being commodities to be managed, rather than people to be noticed and cared for. To the doctor, dear Mr Smith who has just recently been widowed becomes the broken arm in cubicle seven. To the salesperson in the shoe shop, the customer is an unwelcome interruption to her chatter about Saturday night plans. To the pastor, the gathering of uniquely-storied individuals becomes the congregation, or worse still, the crowd.

Today, most of us will see people. I'm not suggesting that we stop and stare at everyone, studying them intently. People who do that are called stalkers. But with God's help, let's take time today to look, notice, and, if appropriate, stop and really see people. Who knows? Our genuine interest might just change a life. Being seen changed mine.

I wish I'd known...
THAT ADDICTIONS DON'T ANNOUNCE THEMSELVES

I've never been to an Alcoholics Anonymous meeting, although I am planning a trip. Most of the gatherings are only open to those who battle with alcohol addiction, but they do welcome interested parties to their occasional 'open' meetings. I'd like to attend one not because I have a problem with the bottle, or because of a voyeuristic fascination, but to pay my respects and learn from their methodology. Addiction is an epidemic in our culture.

There's one part of AA meetings that is particularly well known, and that's the way each person introduces themselves when they get up to share with the rest of the group. Instead of just offering their name, they preface their comments with a stark confession: 'Hello, my name is John, and I'm an alcoholic.' ('Hi John,' responds the group.)

At first glance, this procedure might seem clichéd at best, and negative at worst. Surely the idea behind these support groups is to enable someone who feels hopeless to know that change is possible, that they can emerge from the quicksand of addiction and the lifestyle that has sucked the life from them? Why stay trapped in the negative identity of alcoholism, even after years of sobriety?

But look again. Addiction hides itself behind denial. The compulsive drinker insists that there is no problem; that they just enjoy a drink or five; that everyone needs whiskey with their cornflakes once in a while. They can give it up anytime they like, they say. But they can't. And as long as the self-deception continues, the addiction grows deeper. When we're brave enough to admit that we're sinking – when we realise our vulnerability – then recovery begins. But denial can lead quickly to disaster.

Right from the very early days of being a follower of Jesus, I knew that I was called to freedom. The Bible is a freedom charter. We are no longer helpless prisoners of sin. Through all that Jesus did on the cross, and through the power of the Holy Spirit at work in our lives today, we are the freedom family. And yet, despite all this, it's still easy to live shackled lives.

Addictions don't announce themselves. An email is not automatically dispatched to the person who is systematically abusing alcohol to tell them that they are now, officially, an alcoholic. And perhaps addiction bites us because of isolation. Many Christians struggle on alone, afraid to admit either to God or humans that they are bound, believing they are not good enough to seek His face and that others will reject them. But without outside help, freedom is often not possible.

And the grip of addiction comes in a variety of guises: food, sex, approval and even religion. If statistics are to be believed, there are many Christians who live their lives shackled to addictive behaviour. So we'd do well to pause and ask ourselves a blunt question: are we under the control of anything? Is there a pattern in our lives that is compulsive, and to which we have quietly become addicted? Perhaps it's time to look into the mirror and fully own the reflection that we see, even if there's ugliness in plain sight. And if the person that stares back at us is addiction-free, let's still beware, and realise that however whole and healthy we may be right now, we still have potential to fall headlong.

Over the years, I've watched both prominent and unknown Christians make disastrous choices that have put their lives – and the lives of others around them – on the rocks. When a private scandal becomes public knowledge, I've frequently heard a deafening sound of tut-tutting, and then amazement at the sordid revelation: 'How could they do such a thing? I could never do that.' It's the latter statement that really troubles me – the notion that we are basically good people who could never venture into anything terribly bad. For one thing, we all share a common humanity, and humanity is fallen. Those who are guilty of both minor and major atrocities are related to us; we all have the same streak of inherent sinfulness as any Nazi, any death-row murderer, any terrorist. When we say, 'I could never do that', we place ourselves in great peril. The knowledge that we too are vulnerable should make us ever more vigilant and careful. Perhaps that's why we are told that we should watch when we stand, lest we fall.

The knowledge of our own sinfulness should make us not only more compassionate to others who fail, but more alert and diligent about our own lives today. Those who are blind to the terrible potential of their fragile humanness are surely more likely to crumble in the face of temptation. Some of us have not committed adultery, but it wasn't steely moral fortitude that has saved us. Chances are we simply haven't had the opportunity, and so we remain untested. While we might determine to never fail, we shouldn't conclude that we never *could* fail.

The late, great Charles Colson – himself a man who had known spectacular public failure during the Watergate scandal – records a moment when one man was faced with the potential of his own fallenness. Yehiel Dinur, a survivor of Auschwitz, testified against Adolf Eichmann, the Nazi architect of the Holocaust, during the Nuremberg trials. During the 1961 proceedings, Dinur walked into the courtroom to come face to face with the man responsible for his incarceration in that hellish camp 18 years earlier. Suddenly, a dam broke insider Dinur, and he began to sob uncontrollably. Then he fainted, collapsing in a heap on the floor as the judge yelled for order in the packed courtroom. But Dinur was not overcome by hatred, paralysed by fear, or tormented by horrid memories. He was devastated by the awful realisation that Eichmann was not some godlike, superhuman army officer who had sent so many to their deaths. Eichmann was just an ordinary man, the guy next door. 'I was afraid about myself,' said Dinur. 'I saw that I am capable to do this. I am… exactly like him.'[1]

So, as followers of Christ, let's never forget the stunning potential for beauty that is ours as saints impelled and steadily transformed by the Holy Spirit. But with that, let's never lose sight of the dark potential of our human fragility either. A sober assessment of ourselves will lead us to affirm that, with God's help, we won't – but let's never say that we never could.

---

[1] Cited by Gene A. Getz, *The Measure of a Man: Twenty Attributes of a Godly Man* (Delight, AR, USA: Gospel Light Publications, 2004).

I wish I'd known...
THAT SAYING 'THANK YOU' MEANS A LOT

The conversation had lulled for the little group that had gathered for dinner. We suffered that awkward moment of wordless pause, the clattering of knives and forks on plates suddenly loud. We'd exhausted topics like Brexit, gun control in America, the price of fuel and, as ever, that chap in North Korea, so it was a welcome relief when one of our number decided to suggest a relatively mindless subject: 'Let's talk about our pet peeves.'

For those unfamiliar with this term, 'pet peeves' are those everyday, seemingly inconsequential happenings and habits of others that irritate, set our teeth on edge, or drive us to distraction and murderous thoughts. Everyone quickly chimed in, and nobody had to dig too deep to come up with something. Apparently we humans are easily irritated. Some pet peeves were common, and we nodded our heads in emphatic agreement when they were shared: people who drive too slow, drive too fast, pick their teeth, always disagree, jump the queue, interrupt when we're mid-sentence, or always say, 'yes, but…'. Others cited coughing without covering your mouth, glancing at your phone mid-conversation, or always having a story that trumps everybody else's stories ('Well, if you think that was difficult, let me tell you what happened to me last Thursday…'). All these things definitely niggle.

But while nose-investigation (picking sounds so very crass) is way up there on my own list of do-that-and-I might-just-hurt-you pet peeves, I immediately knew my number one irritant. Scratch that – this particular peeve is way more than irritating. When I come across it, it nudges me into a grey mood, a funk that can last for hours and sometimes even days. It robs me of joy, and pushes me into resentment.

My pet peeve is ingratitude.

I like to think that I'm generous. I enjoy giving, and am blessed with a wife who would give practically everything away if she could. But for reasons that I can't clarify, I just can't stand being taken for granted. I don't want a framed certificate and a round of applause when I push the proverbial boat out, but it matters to me that it is at least acknowledged. Saying 'thank you' costs nothing. And surely it's good for us to express gratitude. Thankfulness is repeatedly mentioned in Scripture, and not because God constantly wants to be told how amazing He is. When we live thankfully in our relationship with God and others, we celebrate that we have been blessed, that we are the receivers of good gifts. And, of course, thanking others can be a surprising blessing to others too.

I learned that when I met Ken. A giant of a man, he is a care assistant at the centre my mother used to attend. Meeting him for a review some time ago, I found myself struggling with tears, which made me feel rather pathetic. The atmosphere in the centre that Ken and his team run is so very kind and welcoming, and the job that he does is so dedicated – so, with stammering words, I simply said, 'Ken, I want you to know how much I appreciate all that you do for my mum. You obviously do an amazing job.'

Ken's jaw dropped. He seemed quite floored by my comment. 'If my team could hear what you just said, they'd all cry,' he responded. 'We often hear complaints. But seldom do we get any appreciation.'

What a sad summary of how ungrateful we can all be. Just as Jesus was astonished that nine out of the ten healed lepers skipped off without a thank-you, so we can forget to express our gratitude, and those who have served us are left feeling that they are taken for granted. In writing to young Timothy, Paul lists ingratitude as a mark of sinful behaviour. How sad it would be if we became people who sang thanksgiving to God for His good gifts, but failed to express gratitude to those beautiful people who, with acts small and great, enhance our lives. 'Thank you' takes so little time, but can have such a massive impact. To touch again on something I mentioned earlier, perhaps we don't notice people enough to thank them.

In confessing our pet peeves around the dinner table that evening, we also acknowledged that the world is not designed to run according to our preferences, and we are responsible for our reactions when others irritate. For inspiration in that department, I turn to the prophet Elijah. Staying with a widow and her sickly son, he had to deal with ingratitude and accusation when her boy died. Elijah had been the catalyst of the food miracle that had saved them, but because hurt people hurt people, she turned on him. And she vented some of her pent-up shame on him too; there must have been a skeleton in her cupboard, because she speculated that Elijah had come to expose her sin.

Perhaps Elijah was tempted to walk out, or give the woman a serious piece of his mind. But instead, he refused to get embroiled in the argument, retired to his room to pray for the lad, and returned him to the widow – alive. Elijah responded to ingratitude with kindness and self-control.

So, if you pick your nose, or don't say thank you in my presence, I'll do my best to behave well.

And by the way, if you are reading this book because you purchased it (and didn't download it from a pirate website, another pet peeve of mine), may I simply say this:

Thank you. I'm grateful.

I wish I'd known...
THAT IT'S OK TO STAY IN THE BOAT WHEN OTHERS WALK ON WATER

It only lasted a few seconds, but he surely recalled it countless times, shaking his head at the remembrance of it.

Peter saw so many mind-boggling sights during his three-year walk with Jesus. Milky-white, opaque, sightless eyes suddenly focused, seeing colours and shapes for the very first time. A stinking corpse, already rancid in the Mediterranean heat, came to life at a word, and then Lazarus sat down for the most unusual supper party in the history of supper parties. Peter's mother-in-law was healed. Mad men driven insane by tormenting spirits were delivered, suddenly in their right mind, and even wanting to join the Jesus team. And then there was the transfiguration; a ringside seat into a time warp, as Moses and Elijah appeared before them for a pre-Calvary conversation with Jesus (and, even more epic, a glimpse of His true glory on that mountaintop).

But then there was that one unforgettable night for Peter, where faith and fear wrestled within him. Fear ultimately triumphed in the tussle, but he'd still experienced the possibility of impossibility. For a few seconds at least, he'd walked on water. That was miracle enough, it being incomprehensible that anyone could stride across even a millpond's flat, watery surface. But the disciples' tiny boat was battling through a major windstorm, with mountainous waves towering over them. Four miles of exhausting rowing had afforded little progress.

They were afraid.

If that wasn't enough, suddenly they caught sight of what looked like a spectre striding across the boiling waves, heading straight for them.

They were very afraid.

And then, once the terrifying figure had come close enough for them to recognise Him as Jesus, Peter came up with a ridiculous idea, absurd in the extreme.

Jesus knows how to walk on waves. Peter would like to try that too. *How about inviting me into the miracle, Lord? Invite me.*

And Jesus did.

What did it feel like for Peter to swing first one leg and then the other over the edge of the boat, and to settle a foot on the churning water, only to discover that it felt firm? Did he hesitate for a few seconds, his mind screaming that this could not be really happening? But somehow, he rested his weight fully on what could never support his weight at all, and he was walking towards Jesus.

Was it a sudden, fierce gust of wind that changed everything, and snatched defeat from the jaws of victory? Or did he look down, like a man trembling on a tightrope, high above an abyss? The buffeting of the wind in his face, the sight of the churning waters...

He was very afraid, and began to sink. Cold water engulfed him as reality came rushing back. Jesus caught him, and gently reproached him for his doubt. Peter didn't drown, and instead climbed back into the boat with Jesus.

And that's where those of us who preach usually leave the

story. Excitedly, we invite our listeners to get out of their boats, figuratively speaking. Take a risk, we say, and do what you can't do. Stretch yourself. Break out of your comfort zone.

But look around that boat. Look past Peter, still dripping wet. There sits the rest of Jesus' team, including Thomas, famous for doubt. (OK, so perhaps you didn't expect him to go for a stroll on the deep.) But look closer, because also sitting in the boat are impetuous hotheads like James and John, those jumpy sons of thunder who had suggested Jesus nuke a Samaritan village. And there's Andrew, sitting over there by the oars, brother to Peter, who might have thought that if his sibling could do something, he'd at least like to give it a try too.

But the fact is that while Peter walked on water, the others didn't. They stayed put, and earned no rebuke for doing so. The vital key for would-be wave-surfers is this: Peter jumped ship – literally – because *Jesus told him to do so.* John Ortberg helps clarify this in observing that this story is more about obedience than it is about risk-taking. Peter is responding to a *command*. Therefore, we are to discern the authentic call of God from our own impulses. As Ortberg says:

> '*Matthew is not glorifying risk-taking for its own sake. Jesus is not looking for bungee-jumping, hang-gliding, day-trading, tornado-chasing Pinto drivers... This is not a story about extreme sports. It's about extreme discipleship.*'[1]

Peter only got out of the boat because he was commanded to. We can't do anything we want to do, but only that which is commanded by Jesus. Where His command is not, our limits are.

I hear someone protest. 'The apostle Paul announces, "I can do all things through Christ who strengthens me,"' someone insists. There you have it. All things. Anything. But look again.

Bluntly, you *can't* do 'anything', and nor can I. I can't fly without tickets, give birth to twins, play the bassoon, or speak Cantonese. If it's Christ who strengthens me, that means that He will surely only strengthen me to fulfill His calling in my life. Instead of constantly telling people that they can do anything, perhaps we should teach more about all of us knowing our limits and spheres.

And look at Paul's personal situation when he said 'I can do all things'. He's under house arrest. Living within enforced limits, he's talking about living contentedly *within* limits, not busting out of them. The man who said he could do all things couldn't go out for an unaccompanied stroll at that point in his life.

But we're soaked in possibility thinking, and it's not just in the Church that we hear this call to do what we can't do.

Walt Disney is generally given the credit for the 'you can do anything' mantra: 'If you can dream it, you can do it' (though he didn't actually say it, an employee did). And depression-era self-help author Napoleon Hill was said to have come up with the phrase, 'Whatever the mind of man can conceive and believe, it can achieve.' It's a lie frequently touted.

Graduating high-school students are often told that they can do anything they dream. It's a relief when someone actually tells the truth. David McCullough, an English teacher, told graduating seniors in Wellesley High School in Massachusetts: 'You are not special. You are not exceptional.' His speech went viral.

Kyle Worley is equally blunt:

'Growing up in America, children consistently hear that they can "be anything they want to be." This promise is usually accompanied by thoughts of grandeur and extraordinary success. Our ambitions and hopes are educated on the premise that to settle for the *ordinary*, which is often equated with what is boring and indicative of a past and inferior time, is beneath us. This hope of becoming something extraordinary trickles down from the rafters of our dreams, where we dwelt as children, into the basement of our hearts, where adults go to think about what could have been and prepare a path to projecting their fallen dreams onto their "fallen" children.'[2]

We drift into the twilight zone of self-deception when we're constantly told to step out, do what we can't do, and go beyond the limit. It's good to know what we can't do. The call to get out of the boat and walk on water is attractive, but sometimes we need to encourage people to grab hold of the oars and stay put, and not least for this reason: when we step out beyond our capacity, we can create carnage.

So how can we avoid stepping out of the boat and drowning when we're not doing so because Jesus is beckoning? One way is to be sober in self-assessment. Hear Paul again: 'do not think of yourself more highly than you ought, but rather think of yourself with sober judgment' (Rom. 12:3). One Greek expositor says that this is a call for us to recognise our limits and respect them. In other words, let's not pretend to be more than we are. Recognise your God-given abilities and use them, but when you come to the edge of your limitations, be willing to say, 'This is too much for me.' And let's ask God for the wisdom to know the difference between a comfort zone and a sphere. We should be willing to step out of the first, and hesitant to go beyond the boundaries of the second. When we step out of a comfort zone, it's an act of faith. When we step beyond a sphere, it's an act of foolishness.

At the feeding of the 5,000, Jesus tried to nudge His disciples out of their comfort zone with the words, 'You give them something to eat'. They didn't understand, and missed the opportunity.

When Peter stepped out of the boat, he was stepping out of a comfort zone – but when he sliced off the high priest's servant's ear, he stepped out of his sphere – becoming a mercenary rather than a disciple. Similarly, he tried to act as advisor to Jesus in suggesting that He should never go to the cross. He stepped beyond his sphere, and got a good telling-off for doing so ('Get behind me, Satan' is certainly a firm rebuke).

Our friends can also help us in discerning our limits, as we nurture truth-telling relationships. Once upon a time, many years ago, I was an occasional worship leader. Thankfully, the day came when a trusted but unsubtle friend told me that worship leading was not really my primary gift, and that the body of Christ would probably let out a collective sigh of relief if I would pack my guitar away for good. I'm glad he spoke up! Recognising what I couldn't do was a painful but enlightening step on the pathway of discovering what I *could* do. The wounds of a friend are faithful, if not always welcome.

Today, you might want to walk on water. But before you hop overboard, you might consider the possibility that it may be far better for you – and for others around you too – to stay in the boat.

---

[1] John Ortberg, *If You Want to Walk on Water, You've Got to Get Out of the Boat* (Grand Rapids, MI, USA: Zondervan, 2001)
[2] Kyle Worley, 'Celebrating the "Ordinary"', written for CBMW.org, 24 July 2013 (accessed January 2018).

I wish I'd known...
THAT SAYING 'SORRY' CAN MEAN NOTHING

Boys will be boys, as they say, and I recall one occasion when my grandsons were busily illustrating that truth. Alex had a toy that he didn't want to share, and Stanley felt that this was a violation of the Christian ethic of selflessness – so he gave his younger brother a slap. Alex didn't feel able at this stage of his spiritual maturity to turn the other cheek, so he gave his brother a slap in response. Much yelling ensued, until our son-in-law Ben intervened, defused the escalating conflict, and then made the demand that parents always make when siblings get into a fuss: 'Now, guys, say sorry to each other.'

Silence. Reluctance. Much shrugging of junior shoulders. Both waited, hesitating because going first with the apology would be tantamount to admitting greater guilt, and that wasn't going to happen.

Finally, the deadlock was broken. Stanley, his face wooden, eyes down on the carpet, mumbled, 'Sorry.' Alex responded with a reciprocal mumble. Neither one looked at the other. And although they did as they were told, this much was obvious: if there were such a thing as an instrument to measure heartfelt sincerity, they would have both registered low on the scale. What was real was their desire to end the telling-off session, and the mouthing of 'sorry' did just that. It's not just children who do this: some of us adults have honed this to a fine art. Saying sorry is a way to end the awkwardness of potential offence, but A.A. Gill laments: 'The British sorry is a prophylactic word. It protects the user and the recipient from the potentially explosive consequences of the truth.'[1]

Ouch.

Elton John famously sang that 'sorry seems to be the hardest word' – and for some, it really is. I recently watched a documentary where a daughter confronted her father about the years of horrendous physical abuse that he'd inflicted upon her mother. The abusive father looked shamed; he shifted around uncomfortably in his seat and admitted that he felt bad, but 'that was then, but this is now. Let's move on,' he said. What he didn't say was 'sorry'. She waited and waited, allowing the awful silence to hang between them, desperate for him to just apologise. As far as I know, she's still waiting.

One of the catchphrases that emerged from the classic movie *Love Story* (1970) was the misguided notion that 'love means never having to say you're sorry', which has to be one of the most ridiculous statements ever made.

But I'm wondering if for some, 'sorry' isn't hard to say, and it's not because love means that we don't have to say it. Rather, we can squander 'sorry'. Like a country that hits an economic crash and discovers that its currency is now next to worthless, surely we can devalue the currency of apology if we use it thoughtlessly and cheaply.

Apparently, the English are especially guilty of apology misuse. Our readiness to apologise for things we haven't done is almost comical, and yet tempered by our unwillingness to apologise for things we *have* done. And sometimes 'sorry' is not about warding off conflict, but just a vanilla expression of politeness; something to make our lives easier.

Being seen to be humble (and being quick to apologise can be an expression of that) is also a great way to look good. In wanting to appear servant-like, we consider that girding our loins with a towel is a tad bit extreme, and so an easier strategy is to live on the edge of apology. In a 2010 study, young Canadians were asked about their 'saying sorry' moments. Many people aged 18 to 25 were 'more interested in impressing others and in advancing through making personal connections in their career and everyday life and therefore are more open to saying "sorry" to keep the relationship positive'.[2]

Even more alarmingly, some even use 'sorry' as a device for repeating their bruising behaviour. The British government has been on a recent campaign to highlight the evils of domestic abuse and discuss the disturbingly high number of people who resort to violence in their closest relationships. No doubt the abuser often says 'sorry' after the punching – but then the pattern continues. 'Sorry' has changed nothing.

I've met people who seem to spend their lives hurting others and then rushing to emotional, apologetic speeches. They consistently bruise with their thoughtless words, hurt with their blundering decisions, but are quick to utter the word 'sorry'. An apology is not a sticking plaster that we can hastily slap on to heal a deep wound, especially when a destructive pattern of behaviour continues.

And sometimes the word 'sorry' can actually be harmful in church circles. I recently endured an awkward prayer gathering where the topic for the evening had been forgiveness, and the preacher suggested that we end the evening by approaching anyone who had offended us and telling them that we had released them from our anger, and that we were sorry for our lingering bitterness. The saddest sight was of a line of people that had formed around one fairly well-known Christian leader, who had obviously managed to upset quite a few people in his time. I thought that perhaps we should have installed one of those 'take a number' contraptions that are found in supermarkets: 'Yes, I'm very glad that you've got that off your chest, but there are a lot of people waiting to confront me here… Number 47, please…'

The practice of informing people that we've been upset with them (sometimes over a period of many years) is dubious at best; these 'confessions' can be a sneaky way of hurting people while feeling pious at the same time. I've had a few people tell me how liberated they felt after getting their hatred for me off their chest – and I've been left feeling devastated as a result.

Not everything has to be sorted out or talked through. Sometimes we need to just keep our irritation and even our sense of offence to ourselves, deal with it in our relationship with God, and move on. A big revelatory confession is not always needed. Not everything requires a big sorting out.

'Sorry' is often just the first step on a meaningful journey. That's why the Bible celebrates godly *sorrow*. There's a sorrow that we can feel just because we've been caught, or are embarrassed about our failure, or grieved because of the consequences of our actions. But true sorrow is but a stepping-stone to real change; it might involve weeping, but when the tears are dried, there's a change of behaviour. Saul wept bitterly over his murderous treatment of David, but all too soon his abusive behaviour returned (1 Sam. 26:2).

Perhaps you're in a relationship where a punch is usually followed up with a tearful apology. You may even have been told that it's your Christian duty to forgive, therefore you have to put up with this abusive lifestyle. But that's just another form of emotional blackmail and manipulation. Sorry can be a hollow word, and a control word too.

We'd do well to learn from the formal Japanese notion of *sunao*, or 'selfless surrender'. In making an apology, Japanese culture demands that the penitent person fully surrenders to the perception of the person that they have wronged, and places themselves at their mercy. Costly indeed.

So let's view the 'sorry' word as a valuable, genuine concession that shouldn't be tossed around and cheapened. Let's not flash it in an attempt to validate our credentials in humility. And whatever we do, let's not use sorry in a way that creates more sorrow.

[1]A.A. Gill, *The Angry Island: Hunting the English* (London: Weidenfeld & Nicolson, 2005)
[2]Cited in an article by Linda Geddes, 'Why do the British say "sorry" so much?', *BBC Future*, 24 February 2016 (accessed January 2018).

I wish I'd known...

THAT TEACHING ISN'T DEEP JUST BECAUSE IT'S CONFUSING

It happened after a communion service at a major conference. It was Sunday morning, and I was attending an all-age worship family service. All went well, except for the fact that the adults had to participate in an endless song *with actions*, which required us to announce that even if we were chimpanzees in the jungle, we would still worship the Lord. We further expressed our determination to be faithful worshippers, should that metamorphosis into the animal kingdom ever occur, as we strutted around making ooh-ooh noises. But it was all good fun, despite our failing to impress some of the children with our chimp impersonations.

And then it was time for the preacher to speak. Given the all-age content of the service up until that point, I thought that he would probably share a familiar story that would be accessible across the ages. Zacchaeus, perhaps, or Jairus' daughter being raised from the dead, which is slightly more palatable than stinky Lazarus staggering out of his rancid tomb in rather grubby grave clothes. Or the little boy Samuel being called by God, only to repeatedly wake up old Eli in the night – an episode that has a smidgen of Monty Python about it.

But there was no mention of the reformed tax collector, little Sam, or the synagogue leader's offspring. Instead, the speaker delivered a 40-minute talk that was not only completely inappropriate for a multi-generational service (it focused on a series of complex theological issues with no apparent practical application), but it was also quite inaccessible and filled with technical language. The children looked bewildered. The adults looked confused. On and on it went, until – surely in answer to the whispered prayers of many, and punctuated by one little chap who stood up and yelled, 'Can we just be chimps again?' – the speaker prayed his closing prayer. The congregation released an almost deafening sigh of relief, and the hapless chap sat down. The person leading the service thanked him warmly for such a wonderful talk, and we all obligingly applauded. (If it's possible for a clap to be insincere, this round of applause was irrefutably hollow.) I wondered how often we Christians lie through our teeth when in public settings. Everyone knew it was a disaster… or so I thought.

Shuffling out of the auditorium, I turned to a friend as we emerged into bright sunlight. 'What on earth was all that about?' I said.

'I'm not sure,' said my friend, also a minister. 'I didn't understand a word of it either, but I think it was really deep teaching.'

My mouth fell open. I couldn't believe it. The suggestion was that deep teaching meant that we would all be at odds to comprehend what was being said. The fact that the sermon was irrelevant, ill-timed, and void of any practical application for a human being (or chimp) of any age meant that it had to surely be substantial. Ridiculous.

Some Christians like things to be 'deep'. Someone who is 'deeply spiritual' probably prays at unearthly hours when even angels are sleeping. But 'depth' can also be used as a highly effective weapon, a powerful missile in the armoury of anyone who likes to criticise without fear of contradiction. 'The teaching in this church is just not deep enough,' snorts the irate congregant, a look of measured indignation on their scowling face. 'The preaching is so superficial.' Christian leaders fear comments like these, because there is simply no way to question whether the critic is right or not. Who is to say what is deep, and what is not? There's no meter to plug in during the sermon to scientifically measure how many spiritual fathoms the content contains. And it gets worse.

In some church circles, it seems that the better the teacher you are, the more likely it is that some will think you're superficial, because you take what is complex and make it accessible and clear. Some conclude, therefore, that you're not very learned, and your skill in communication is touted as evidence that you are shallow. The likelihood of you being called superficial is heightened if you use humour in your communication, because if people understand you and enjoy the experience, there must be something wrong (according to some furrowed-browed killjoys).

I'm heartened by the fact that the greatest teacher in history told delightful little stories to illustrate truth, and sometimes to send His listeners on a hunt for further truth. Did Jesus use humour? I'm reliably informed that all that talk of camels squeezing through the eye of a needle would have caused a giggle, although the gag might be thousands of years out of date by now. Some have actually asked if Jesus ever laughed, which surprises me, seeing as He was such a popular party guest, and not just because He was rather good with wine. Children rushed to Him. They would not be quite as enthusiastic if He moped around as a miserable, wide-eyed Pharisee. Surely story and humour were part of His life, and were tools used to help people understand what on earth the man from heaven was talking about.

So beware of teaching that confuses and makes the Christian faith complicated and even beyond reach. Pray for those who teach and preach in your local congregation, because theirs is a heavy responsibility: to shed light on God-breathed Scripture, and use their teaching gift to make truth accessible.

Deep doesn't mean confusing.

I wish I'd known...
THAT BEING A PROFESSIONAL CHRISTIAN IS DANGEROUS

Roger Forster is a leader I've admired for decades. Not only does he have a brain the size of a planet, but he's kind. Unsullied by scandals that have dogged higher profile Christian leaders, he and his wife are rightly respected veterans of the faith. I've read Roger's books and heard him teach many times too, but there's one throwaway statement that he made in a leadership forum that has stayed with me. It's simple, but profound. Talking to a group of so-called 'full-time' Christian leaders, he pinpointed a very real challenge: 'The difficulty for all of us is this,' he mused. 'God is our job.'

And he's right. There are particular perils for those who are in ministry, not least this – we can end up performing a work function rather than engaging in a daily, living faith. There's an old joke about a young man who was awakened by his mother on a Sunday morning. 'Get up, son, it's time to go to church.' Turning over and pulling the pillow over his head, the young man protested, as many young men do when church is the next item on the Sunday morning agenda.

'I hate it. I don't want to go,' he groaned.

'Why ever not, son?' asked his enquiring mother, sweetness laced with a tinge of God-is-going-to-get-you-if-you-don't-get-up-right-now.

'Well, nobody likes me there. The sermons are boring and irrelevant. I get nothing out of the worship. Give me one good reason why I need to go there today.'

'That's simple, son,' said his mother. 'You're the pastor.'

It might just be an old chestnut that ministers share when they get together, but it illustrates a point. When those of us who work for the Church go to church, it's not about whether we actually want to go, or whether our heart is in it – it's part of our job description, and we're therefore expected to perform accordingly.

I use the word 'perform' deliberately, because there will be times when leaders have to do just that. I tread carefully here. Jesus denounced the Pharisees as hypocrites, a word that comes from the term *hypokritees*, which was the name for a group of travelling actors. They were skilled thespians who made audiences gasp, laugh and cry out loud, thousands of years before computerised special effects or Hollywood. As the actors plied their craft onstage, their vividly painted, grossly exaggerated masks made them look so convincing. As a boy, it's possible that Jesus might have seen them in action – the remains of a nearby theatre have been discovered in the area where He was raised. In Jesus' day, there were also some who used religion as a performance script, their lives a well-rehearsed, pious masquerade. The street corners became their stage as they prayed loudly with trembling voices and elaborate vocabulary. They invested heavily in the wardrobe department, with their dress-to-impress gowns and dangling phylacteries – leather-bound Scriptures tied to their hair. They were consummate performers, and their lives were a sham, which is why I use the word 'perform' with caution.

But anyone who stands in public to lead or speak has to deliver a level of performance. The sermon has to be preached, even if the preacher is going through something of a faith crisis. The congregation don't want to be told that their leader is having a rough week, and therefore the sermon is cancelled (actually, in some cases, perhaps they do…). Self-disclosure and vulnerability are important qualities for all preachers, but people don't want them to download their current angst on them every week.

I've struggled with this at times, feeling that my emotions don't match my words. But I don't have to feel it to mean it.

My vintage friend Adrian Plass has helped me with this. Years ago, he told me that our feelings are not the barometer of our spirituality. He went on to share that when he feels uncertain, unaware of God, and is tempted to step away from his ministry because he feels like a fraud, he remembers that while his life should reflect his message, he is but the postman – the imperfect messenger. This was liberating news to me. Of course, there are perils here too – when we preach one thing and then deliberately develop a pattern that is totally at odds with what we're calling others to do, we've stepped away from being performing messengers and stepped into becoming performing hypocrites. But the reality is that our lives will never perfectly match the aspirations expressed in our sermons. What matters is that we are genuinely heading in the right direction. Leadership is about setting an example, but that's not the same as projecting an image. When we do the latter, not only are we frauds, but we discourage our hearers because we give the false impression that we are not living in the same reality as them.

Another snare for leaders is the thought that we are above living according to basic principles of good conduct. I've mentioned it elsewhere, but Bill Hybels has talked about the day when he realised that he'd been deluded into thinking that good behaviour was just to be preached about, and not lived out in his own experience –

and this was brought to his attention when a staff member left him a note about his parking.

Dashing into his office at the church, and in a hurry, Hybels had parked for a few moments in the 'no parking' zone. One of the church maintenance staff apparently remarked that 'there was another jerk in the no parking area'. The leader of their maintenance crew decided to confront the issue, and left a kind (but blunt) note telling the senior pastor that his parking habits were not helpful. Instead of pulling rank, Hybels was grateful for the rebuke, realising that he was not to be the exception to the rules, but an example of how life should be lived – in church, in finances, in sexual ethics, and… in parking. In Hybels' own words: 'we all need people like my staff member to hold us accountable in even the small matters. Because when we keep the minor matters in line, we don't stumble over the larger ones.'[1]

My respect for Hybels shot up when I learned that, with all of his success, he remains willing to be checked by those he signs a paycheck for.

We can also start to think that the sermon is for others, and not us. Sometimes I catch myself thinking about a list of folks whom I think really need to hear a particular message, only to then realise that I have forgotten that God might be challenging *me* through His Word.

I recently realised I was subconsciously excluding myself – and it was during a service where I was the preacher. Just before the meeting closed, someone came forward and mentioned that the leaders had sensed that God wanted to heal someone with tinnitus (persistent ringing in the ears). This malady can be torment. I know, because I've suffered from it for some years now. But my initial response was to think that this 'word of knowledge' was for someone else in the church, not me. I had counted myself out.

Eventually, I presented myself for prayer. The prayer team member, somewhat under pressure because the visiting preacher was asking for prayer, poured his heart out in petition. I didn't get healed. But I did learn to count myself in.

So pray for those who have the blessing and responsibility of leadership, that today, when it comes to experiencing grace, living in obedience, and being accountable, they too will count themselves in. Being a leader is a privilege. But it should carry a health warning too.

---

[1] Bill Hybels, 'But I'm an Exception!', www.christianitytoday.com/pastors/1988 (accessed January 2018).

I wish I'd known...
THAT GOD HAS A HOBBY

I always have mixed emotions when hearing about other people's hobbies. I experience a combination of slight envy and bemused bewilderment when others share how they spend their free time. I am mildly jealous of one friend in particular, who is passionate about carp fishing. I covet the thrill that he feels when pitching his tiny one-man tent on the mushy bogland by a mosquito hotel of a lake. He sits there for no less than three days, undisturbed, unwashed, and loving every moment of it. When at last he hooks a carp (some of which he has caught before, and knows by name), he takes a selfie with the wide-eyed fish lovingly cradled in his arms, and then releases it back into the murky depths. I can't decide whether to emulate him, or encourage him towards psychotherapy.

Something similar happens when I'm around golfers. I loathe the game, not least because I am so useless at it (being possessed of a spasm rather than a swing). The last time I played, I got teamed up with some Japanese gentlemen who were very, very good at golf, but about as good with English as I am with the Japanese language (where I am limited to a single word: sushi). After just seven holes of me gouging great clods of turf out of previously pristine greens, taking 15 shots on a par three hole (and usually missing the wretched ball altogether), they both fled, after much apologetic bowing. I haven't played since.

I don't really have any hobbies. I am rather partial to a glass of wine, but that's not something to get too passionate about. People who do can end up joining a club with others who share their enthusiasm. It's called rehab.

But more than 40 years of Christian life and ministry have taught me that God does have a primary hobby. It's called redemption. Let me explain. In using the word redemption, I'm not talking about the wondrous act of cosmic rescue achieved at the cross. In a way that none of us can fully understand (but have historically argued about quite a lot), Jesus redeemed us at Calvary. This was the greatest work of all works, as the creator became liberator. I'm talking about God's amazing ability to bring good out of what was bad – in a word, *redeeming*. The master of turnaround, He doesn't just forgive what He was not the architect of, but takes the myriad muck-ups and messes that we mucked-up and messed-up humans make, and brings something beautiful out of them. He mines treasure out of our trashier episodes. I'm not being irreverent in tagging this as God's hobby. A hobby is often an unusual action that brings great pleasure to the hobbyist. I believe God is especially thrilled with His redeemed, recycled masterpieces, of which there are many.

Whiney, petulant Israel huffed and puffed and stamped her national foot, demanding a human king, which was never the plan. But out of that rebellious uprising came not only the insecure disaster that was Saul, but also golden-boy, Goliath-toppling King David. But like all humans, he had feet of clay. David hooked up with Bathsheba, and added murder to the sin of adultery, by having her innocent, righteous husband killed off, the casualty of a royal conspiracy. Yet out of the eventual marriage between David and Bathsheba came Solomon, the greatly celebrated wise man. And from his line came the wisest and greatest royal, Jesus, the King of kings Himself.

Later, Judas sold Jesus out, religious barons connived to bring Him down, and the brutal Romans did their worst – but this vile morass led to the greatest turnaround in human history as the cross, the instrument of death, became the tree of life, its eternal fruit available to all.

And God's redemptive hobby can be traced in smaller triumphs. White-hot zealous types stumble and fall – but become more compassionate and tolerant because of their tumble. Bewildered believers who once had faith figured out suddenly hit a wall of question marks. In trusting through the unexplained, they make friends with mystery. Suffering makes an unwelcome house call, and although nobody in their right mind would actually request a visit, solid gold faith is forged by the pain.

Few of us can look back on the pathway we've trod without any regret, and those without regrets might just be deluded. But let's be assured of this: we serve the God of the turnaround. If we have our own horrible histories, not only does He wipe away their stain, but He can bring beauty out of the ashes of our mistakes and sins too.

I wish I'd known...
THAT EVERYONE NEEDS SOMEONE TO SING THE BASSLINE

It was one of those faintly ridiculous and mildly hilarious Christian gatherings (which always seem to cheer me up no end). I spend so much time in Christian services, meetings, conferences, retreats and celebrations that I sometimes feel sorry for God. He apparently attends them all – one of the drawbacks of omnipresence, perhaps.

I was particularly enjoying this meeting, not least because I had absolutely no responsibility in it. I spend my life waiting for the nod that signals that it's time for me to preach, which means that I can rarely just enjoy singing in worship – my mind is flitting around, thinking of what I'm about to say, and I'm invariably fiddling with my iPad, making last-minute adjustments before delivering the talk. And then, when I'm the one bringing the sermon, there's a consistent arrangement that I have to live with: the fact that I always have to listen to me. I've listened to myself blithering on quite a few times over the years, and am occasionally tempted to tell myself to belt up (though that would be rather odd). But at this particular service, I was looking forward to the luxury of listening to someone else.

The worship leader, apparently nine years old (I exaggerate, but he did seem impossibly young), was leading a rather lilting song, but he had chosen the wrong key. I know this because all the men were trying to sing in a lower octave, but it was just too deep for most of us, which meant that there were moments in the song when we had to go up into falsetto mode. The result was the sound of a notational symphony (cacophony, more like) where the men alternated between gruff, off-key bass tones and high-pitched squealing. If any passing angels had noise-cancelling headsets built into their halos, they were certainly using them now. The worship song had at least 58 verses (actually six, but that's how it felt), and I was trying very hard not to laugh out loud.

When things go wrong during services, leaders often notice people watching them to see what their reaction is. I so wanted to guffaw, but it would not have been appropriate, so I busied myself with the thought pattern that I use when wanting to not giggle: I thought of painful death, of public shame, and then resorted to my old standby, which involves me being eaten alive by a marching army of Honduran fire ants. That took the smile off my face.

But it was then that I heard a voice behind me, a deep, resonant voice manfully belting out the lower bassline of the song. It was my friend, Dick Foth. I decided to take a break from the shrieking, and just listen to him. He has a nice voice. He's not going to fill any concert halls, but the man can sing. Dick's speaking voice is rather brilliant too: a one-time radio presenter, he has the perfect vocal timbre and texture for that medium. (I have been told that when it comes to radio, I have the perfect face for it...)

But as I tuned in to Foth, a realisation dawned that sparked immediate gratitude: Dick has been a bassline in my life. Strong, solid and substantial, his friendship, together with that of his wife Ruth, has undergirded my faith and helped keep the rhythm going for quite some time.

I first met him 30 years ago. A new immigrant to America, I was feeling homesick and bewildered, not so much by the culture but by the church where I served as an associate pastor. Everything was different from church life in the UK. Men gathered for Saturday morning prayer meetings where they would laugh and joke about the football game they'd watched yesterday, but then instantly move into wailing and sobbing the moment someone said, 'Let's pray' – and then the moment the corporate 'Amen' was sounded, it was back to levity and sports again. I couldn't understand why God apparently wanted us to howl and cry all the time. Repentance was big, and we did it every Sunday morning, owning the shame of the sins of the planet. I was bewildered, because God seemed very tetchy, if not downright angry. Suffering from suffocating homesickness, I wondered if it was time for my family and me to return to Blighty.

And then I went off for a men's weekend retreat. I wasn't hopeful, because the place was packed with chaps sporting massive beards, who wore baseball caps and check-flannel shirts. It looked like a lumberjack convention. I didn't have a flannel shirt, all hats perch on my head in a way that looks awkward, and last time I tried to grow a beard, my face resembled a guinea pig's backside. When I opened my mouth to speak, my British accent gave me away, and so now I was the novelty item: a beardless, flannel-less, cap-less, hapless foreigner. Booking homebound flights seemed like a very sensible thing to do.

Until the speaker for the weekend stood up, that is. It was Foth. He had an endless supply of fascinating stories. He didn't seem to think that God was irritated with us all; on the contrary, when he talked, I felt like God was really rather delighted to know me. I can't remember a thing he preached about (people often say this of preaching and preachers, which is just *so* encouraging), but there was something about him that thawed the spiritual chill that had crept into my soul, and warmed my heart towards being in America again. I decided to stay.

That was the last I saw of Dr Foth, until I was asked to speak at Bethany Bible College in California, where Dick was then serving as President. As chapel speaker, it was my privilege to have dinner with the president. Dick was wrestling with a migraine so the dinner was probably a chore for him, but I was thrilled.

And then, years later, Dick and Ruth decided to relocate to Fort Collins, Colorado, and be part of Timberline Church, where I serve as a teaching pastor. He joined our team, and although his role has morphed so that he is not part of the day-to-day operation anymore, he and Ruth still make a significant contribution to the life of our church.

And so my bassline-singing friend is a regular part of my life now. Over breakfast recently, I somewhat tearfully told him about this piece that I am writing.

Thanks for singing the bassline, Dick. And thanks for keeping him in tune, Ruth. Please keep singing along for many, many years to come.

I wish I'd known...
THAT OPENING DOORS IS A GOOD THING TO DO

Being a man, and trying to be polite with it, can be challenging these days. On a crowded train, I'm never sure whether I should offer my seat to a lady. Will she smile and thank me, or screamingly announce to the entire carriage that I'm a patronising misogynist? The dilemmas continue. Upon opening a door for a woman the other day and saying, 'After you,' I was treated to an icy glare rather than a nod of appreciation. I wasn't suggesting that she was incapable of turning the handle; I just thought a good-mannered gesture might be welcome. I was wrong. And it was awkward. But I like people who open doors for others. One of those people changed my life.

I've just mentioned how, 30 years ago, my family relocated to a rather isolated area of America, a place where real men drove trucks, wore baseball caps, chewed gum, and went deer hunting (some even wore camouflage pyjamas, ensuring that they would be suitably dressed should they ever encounter Bambi in their sleep). We were bewildered and felt very alone. The culture was so very foreign to us. I've mentioned that my friend Dick Foth was a lifeline, but another family rescued us from stifling loneliness too. Separated from our own kin during seasons like Christmas, Jack and Darlene Faulkner welcomed us in as if we were their own. A particularly scary Christmas (which included waiting for the verdict on a cancer scare) was lightened by laughter around their table, and our children learned to water-ski on the wake left behind their speedboat. Years later, we're still grateful for the legacy of their friendship and kindness.

Then we relocated to a city 180 miles distant – and that's where we met Milton and Barbara. They opened the doors of their home to us, literally. Needing somewhere to live while we looked for a house to rent, they gave our young family far more than a space in their home: their gift was a place in their hearts. With grandchildren thousands of miles across the ocean, they adopted our family. Milton hailed from the Deep South, and with his white moustache and gentle drawl, he looked like a cast member of *Gone with the Wind*. We didn't know many people in our new homeland, and so they opened up their friendship circle to include us too. Their folks became our folks. We were family, and we still are.

A few months ago, Milton discovered that he was going to see Jesus rather sooner than he had anticipated. An inoperable cancer meant that he had very little time to live. He asked his doctor, a mutual friend, to call us with the news. We were shattered.

A few minutes later, we chatted with him on the phone. That warm, southern tone was unwavering. We told him how much we loved him, and gave him firm instructions that however much he was anticipating heaven, we needed him to hang on until we could get to see him and Barbara. A sumptuous farewell dinner was planned, a feast to celebrate his life before his death and homecoming. (And yes, we were praying for healing, but making preparations to say goodbye in case the healing wasn't to happen.)

Before we made that phone call, I scrambled for words to comfort and encourage; words which were completely unnecessary. 'There's no problem here, Brother Jeff,' he said. 'We're good, everything is fine. I'm going to a place where time doesn't exist as we know it. That means that very soon, we'll all be together again. It's just that I'm getting there ahead of you. But don't worry, I'll be waiting, and I'll hold heaven's door open for you.'

We had that farewell meal, which was beautiful, and not just because Barbara's marvellous culinary gifting has not paled. We remembered days long gone; we laughed, we cried, and then Kay and I knelt before Milton and asked for his blessing. With the care that characterised him for decades, he spoke with special kindness about the way that Kay had stood faithfully beside me, ever supportive through the years. He had special words of encouragement for her. Once again, he opened the door of unexpected kindness and recognition.

I don't know who heaven's doorman is. Tradition has it that St Peter, the fisherman turned key-holder, is parked at the pearly gates, and I don't think he's nervous that Milton is after his job. But what I do know is this: in life, Milton has been a door-opener, and he wants to continue in the job. And rather than just admiring and celebrating my lovely friend, I'd like to follow his example and be someone who opens doors for others – doors to joy, to opportunity, to laughter, to understanding – I'd like be a door-opener myself. Following a Jesus who calls Himself 'the door' as well as 'the way', I'd like to be like Christ.

'I have set before you an open door,' Jesus said to one of the seven churches of Revelation. And in a way that none of us can ever fully grasp, Jesus opened the door to eternity with God at the cross. He who was first put Himself last and, beckoning sinful humanity, He gestured with open arms and whispered, 'After you.'

My friend Milton, at last, has gone home. His suffering is ended.

Pain was a constant companion as his life here drew to a close, but he faced it with faith and courage. When I phoned him a few days before his death, effectively to say goodbye, he was amazed that I was making transatlantic contact. 'Well, bless your heart, Brother Jeff. I can't believe it. It's so good to hear your voice.' The pain was so intense that he dropped the phone during the conversation. And lovely Barbara stood by his side through it all.

Milton is with Jesus now, and one of these days, when the millions gather as we all see the glorious Christ face to face, I'm going to track Milton down, and share that familiar hug.

I wondered how I might find him – one man among the many millions. Perhaps that warm, southern drawl would stand out. But then I realised.

I know just where I'll find you, Brother Milton: you'll be right there at the door.

I wish I'd known...
THAT IT'S OK FOR CHURCH TO BE BORING

I looked around. I was the guest speaker in a large, successful church, and the service was hopping – literally. The congregation were well into the songs, and a gaggle of enthusiastic teens had rushed to the front of the auditorium to the edge of the stage, where they were dancing to the high energy tunes. Onstage, the worship team were technically brilliant, the graphics on the huge screen behind them stunning. Each member of the band (there were about ten of them) looked like they had stepped out of a fashion magazine. Fabulous teeth that facilitated gleaming smiles, the ladies all young and beautiful, and the chaps all appeared to be sporting six-pack abs and fruit-of-many-workouts biceps. (I wondered if slightly overweight, average-looking folks were banned from the platform, but surely the 'ugly' quota would be more than fulfilled once I got up to preach.)

Everything looked great, but inwardly, something still wasn't right with me. I often feel like that in church. Everyone else seems totally caught up in the holy moment, and I catch myself fretting; distracted; questioning; anxious. I feel more like a refugee than a local. Perhaps you know the feeling.

What's wrong? I asked myself. This church had grown from a fledgling plant to a thriving congregation of 2,000 people in ten years, and had planted other congregations in that fruitful decade. I didn't know the pastor well, but he came across as an authentic leader and a brilliant communicator. So what was up? I wondered if I was struggling because this was the third service of the morning. I had sat through all the songs, announcements, the 'spontaneous' witty asides twice already, and perhaps this was just beginning to feel a little redundant. But that was not it. My home church has three Sunday morning services, which means that I get to hear myself three times over when I preach. I'm used to repetition.

And then I identified the source of my vague disquiet.

These are great people. The music is wonderful. And, beneath the surface, they are truly committed to the gospel – the financial giving of the church shows that they mean business and are willing to sacrifice to fulfill their mission. It's all good... but... it's all just *too exciting*. I couldn't attend this church regularly, because I can't be that thrilled about being a Christian that regularly. Being ecstatic about being a follower of Jesus on a weekly basis is just beyond me.

As the thought registered, the worship leader stepped up a gear in terms of exhortation, yelled that Jesus was awesome, and with a hint of rebuke in his voice, commanded the now sweaty congregation to dance more, shout louder, clap together, because Jesus was worth it. Inwardly, I groaned.

Now don't misunderstand me. Despite my 61 years, I can shout and clap and even bop with the best of them, even if my dancing does look a little uncoordinated and people have been known to want to call for medical assistance when I break into my jerky, frenetic moves. I love to see a congregation giving their best when they praise the Lord. Sullen, spectator churches depress me.

But I worry when church *has* to always be exciting. When every service has to be a breakthrough, when every gathering has to result in an eye-popping, life-altering encounter with God, and when we have to be excited all the time, surely some unhealthy traits emerge.

First off, life isn't always exciting. On the contrary – I recently spoke to a young widow whose 35-year-old husband had just passed away following a brave, five-year battle with multiple brain tumours. She's trusting all right, but she's far from excited. There's the danger that we reduce faith to having excited feelings, and then when those feelings fail to appear, we wonder where God has gone.

And then there's the problem that looms if every service has to be awesome. Quite simply, we can end up faking it, over-egging what happens because we're desperate for a result.

Surely sometimes church can be predictable. We get together, sing our songs, pray our prayers, open the great Book, ponder its meaning, affirm our faith, and go home. No mountaintop transfiguration experience required, just the people of God huddling together and reminding each other that they are the people of God, and that Jesus is still alive.

Surely we should make allowances for church to be rather 'boring' sometimes? The Early Church must have had at least a few services where they weren't dancing on the tables. Some of their gatherings were punctuated by deep disagreements. And on one glorious occasion, the apostle Paul droned on for so long that a hapless young chap fell asleep and tumbled out of a window. OK, so they raised him up (that bit was exciting) and the slumber was explained by the lulling warmth of oil lamps burning rather than the apostle being tedious, but it happened nonetheless.

Boredom is part of tenacious relationships. Not every conversation with a trusted friend will necessarily be exhilarating. Marriage isn't scintillating every day. Can't the same be true of the collective relationships that we call church?

Recently, there's been a call for worship songs that more accurately reflect the different seasons of life. There's been a dearth of 'songs of lament' that can be used to express struggle, doubt and pain. While I think such songs would be challenging to write ('Let's all stand together and sing number 47: *I'm naffed off, how about you?*'), surely there should be some songs that are appropriate for when a national disaster is announced, or that can express uncertainty, fear, or despair. The great songbook of the Bible, the book of Psalms, contains plenty of these statements; frequently the psalmist asks, why, how long, and even 'God, where have you gone?' Can we not create songs that express the full texture of life here on this broken planet?

Perhaps I should start a new organisation called the International Federation of Occasionally Boring and Predictable Churches. That's silly, I know. Nobody would join. But we could at least give each other permission to truthfully say that life is not an endless hop, skip and jump, and that, at times, although we're still trying to follow Jesus, we're dragging our feet as we do so. Weekly exuberance is therefore not always required. Faithfulness is a fruit of the Spirit; excitement is not.

I wish I'd known...
THAT GOD ISN'T ENDLESSLY CHATTY

It's a frustrating moment. You're having an important conversation with a friend on your mobile when suddenly the line goes dead, usually at the critical moment when they're just about to tell you that the baby has been born, the stock market has collapsed, or that chap in charge of North Korea has pushed a shiny button. Frantic, you yell into the phone: 'Hello? Helllllllooo… Are you there?!' – when it's patently obvious that they're not. Perhaps you even shake the phone, as if agitating a digital chip will cause it to function more efficiently. (It does not.) Finally, you resign yourself to reality. The call has dropped, and you're left with nothing but the ominous sound of silence. Irritating.

After 40 years of following Jesus, I've heard countless claims that God has spoken to people. And I'm not denying that He does. He *has* spoken to me – with life-altering results – on a number of occasions. The Bible lists numerous examples of God speaking to humans. He talks. It's just that I'm not convinced that He is as talkative as some people make out, and when we suggest otherwise, a number of things happen.

When God is painted as someone who is endlessly conversational, faith can be trivialised. If the King of the universe can tell me where to find a parking space, could He not also whisper a cure for cancer, a plan to tackle global warming that everyone (regardless of hairstyles) will sign up to, or a way to deal with those monstrous, flag-waving terrorists? Of course, in the face of the world's problems, any report of God speaking to us first-world folks can seem strange, and if He is truly interested in helping His people park efficiently, then who am I to question? But I often find myself wishing that the content of God's conversation with Christians would be just a bit more weighty.

Let's also consider those who don't seem to have a super-fast broadband connection to an endlessly chatty heaven, feeling guilty about their apparent lack of hearing – what is wrong with them?

Silence can indicate stony silence – an attitude behind or a reason for the silence. We've upset the other party, who aren't talking to us. We're being ignored, shut out, or so we feel. In times past, I've told others that I've found God to be quieter than I anticipated, only to be informed, sometimes tersely, that I just don't listen hard enough. Thanks a lot; I'm glad I shared.

Anyone who has been around Christianity for long knows that foolishness is often justified by tossing down the ace card in the believer's pack – the 'God told me...' move. When we insist that we are acting in response to a divine command, we quickly shut down the possibility of being told that we're wrong. God has stamped our plans with His approval, we declare. Who are others to disagree?

Discerning the voice of God isn't always easy. I'm encouraged by that story of young Samuel, who, when woken up by the voice of God, repeatedly woke up Eli. He heard a voice, but was confused about the source.

I recently heard a preacher announce that God is always talking to us, 24/7. We need to listen more. But that's surely a ludicrous statement. What can God possibly want to chatter on about endlessly? Imagine being around any person who never, ever stopped talking. Be honest – they wouldn't be your friend for long.

Of course, there's a pendulum-swing reaction to the craziness, and that comes when we are automatically concerned about the mental health of anyone who says, 'God said...'. But these days, I'm becoming more content with the sound of silence. It reminds me that this is not all that there is; that a day is coming when our blurred vision of Jesus, myopic because we see Him by faith, will be corrected: we will see Him as He is, and hear Him clearly, undistracted by the noise of life this side of eternity. The silence draws me back to the strong, secure voice of Scripture. I'm nudged to consider that His voice might be discovered in unexpected places, like that kind email I received, or that walk in the country. And I'm heartened by the late, great Oswald Chambers' encouragement that sometimes God trusts us with silence.

But let's not allow this admission to block our ears. While we are not unnerved by the silence, still we posture ourselves for the possibility of His voice. We remember that it was young Samuel who prayed, 'Speak, Lord, for your servant is listening.' While frequent silence no longer causes me anxiety, when He wants to break it, I want to be all ears.

I wish I'd known...
THAT DOUBTERS CAN BE HEROES – JUST BY SHOWING UP

They're days that are consistently tinged with irritation. We generally refer to them as *one of those days*. You wake up with a headache; discover that the dog made a midnight snack of your new Ray-Bans; miss the bus to work; and discover that your boss is actually a werewolf, thinly disguised as a human being. Later in the day, which is layered with further minor frustrations, you're asked how you're doing. You make it official, and mumble, 'OK, I suppose. Just having one of those days.' We all have them.

Thomas, the disciple infamous for his capacity for doubt, had 'one of those days' when he missed that meeting where the resurrected Jesus showed up. Who knows what he was up to that caused him to miss one of the greatest episodes in human history? Was he working on his taxes? Visiting an elderly aunt? Lunching with an old friend? Whatever it was, it caused him to miss that meeting of all meetings.

And now, as the other disciples excitedly chatter about the awesome experience they've just had, Thomas stoically assumes a posture not unlike that of Victor Meldrew, muttering, 'I don't believe it.' He insists that unless he can be convinced that Jesus really is alive – by sticking his fingers into His wounds – then unbelief is the barren place where he is going to park, *so there*. Thus the Christian Church, always quick on the draw with the labelling machine, has dubbed him 'doubting Thomas', which I think is a tad unfair. He certainly did doubt – Jesus gently rebuked him for it – but he was also a brave man, who had shown willingness to die with Jesus if necessary.

Because of his doubting, Thomas is unlikely to be a winner in the 'I'm a disciple, get me out of here' popularity contest. Peter, impetuous and fragile, usually wins hands-down every time. The water-walking fisherman (whose sprint across the surf was terminated by a bolt of fear, as we've seen) is someone we can so easily associate with. I sometimes picture him hop-scotching behind Jesus on one foot, because so often he had the other foot firmly planted in his mouth.

James and John might be favourites with the more macho types who like action thrillers, seeing as they showed an indecent enthusiasm for violence and fiery judgment.

Andrew might be a favourite of some, because he was such a people person, immediately introducing his brother Peter to Jesus and then not getting irritated when his brother got nicknamed 'The Rock'. I confess to finding him slightly irritating, with his gift of stating the obvious. Sharing the insight that a lunch of five loaves and two fishes would not go far in feeding 5,000 chaps (plus women and children) is a prime example.

But strange though it seems, I'd like to give a shout-out to Thomas as an unlikely hero.

And the reason is this: for Thomas, one of those days turned into one of those weeks. The repeated chatter between those who had seen Jesus must have been tortuous, setting Thomas' teeth on edge. We read the story of another appearance of Jesus to Thomas and so we know the happy ending, but for a while, he had no clue that this would happen. He had no promise that Jesus would ever appear again in a similar fashion. He may well have missed the meeting of his life. A whole week went by: seven days for him in the shadowlands.

But then Jesus arrived again, and this time Thomas was there. Still showing up; his doubts unresolved; his insecurities lingering; he was there. And for that reason, he is wonderful inspiration. Woody Allen famously said that 90% of success is showing up, and Thomas did. I don't think we give him enough credit for doing so. Thomas is surely the patron saint of those who are steering through the seasons when faith seems ludicrous, but they still show up regardless.

Sometimes Christians go through wilderness seasons of doubt, and distance themselves from their churches. The songs feel hollow, the prayers seem meaningless, and they may even feel hypocritical because of their faith crisis. *Surely*, they reason, *it's better to stay away*. And that's wrong. Fellowship can give us a source of strength when the going gets tough. Unable to pray much, we allow ourselves to be carried by the prayers of others. Liturgy gives us words of faith when life renders us speechless. The Church is not the gathering of the strong, but the place where we huddle to find strength. Thomas showed up.

And Thomas ended bravely, apparently martyred by spears at the command of an Indian king. His willingness to die for Jesus was no hollow promise.

So hooray for Thomas. And if you're trusting God and still clinging to Christian community through one of those days, weeks, or even – God love you – one of those years, then a sincere, heartfelt hooray for you too.

I wish I'd known...
THAT A REAL FRIEND WILL TELL YOU THE TRUTH

As a singer, she was a phenomenal success, packing out New York's prestigious Carnegie Hall. A chart-topper as the best-selling artist for her recording company, she worked very hard for her success, hiring a renowned vocal coach to help hone her technique. Her friends cheered her on, celebrating her unique gift.

There was just one problem. She couldn't sing. The subject of a recent film starring Meryl Streep and Hugh Grant, Florence Foster Jenkins has become renowned for being the world's worst opera singer. According to one rather cutting historian, 'No one, before or since, has succeeded in liberating themselves quite so completely from the shackles of musical notation'. Ouch.

Apparently oblivious to the fact that her audiences actually gathered to quietly mock her, she was consistently flat – sometimes off-key by as much as a semitone. With her poor diction, she massacred foreign-language lyrics. But undeterred, she kept on singing, while her fans sniggered behind their hands. Hers is a tragic, pathetic story, made possible because nobody loved her enough to tell her the truth.

Something similar happens in churches where a genuine

commitment to encouragement has distilled into hollow flattery – where we so want to cheer people on that we end up barking them up the wrong tree, nudging them to do what God has not called or equipped them to do. Someone preaches a fairly mediocre sermon, and is promptly told that it was brilliant. Where the gifts of the Spirit are operated, a seriously dodgy prophecy is shared on a Sunday morning: the congregation-wide, mass clenching of buttocks means that everyone knows the God of the universe most likely has *not* spoken, but for fear of crushing the would-be prophet – or worse still, offending him or her – everyone stays tight-lipped. The emperor's clothes remain unruffled.

There's a greater danger of this when any kind of constructive criticism is viewed as negative or even divisive. Nervous of being tagged as a dissenter, people nod their head and blindly affirm. Not only does this dilute the possibility of quality control, but it devalues the currency of genuine encouragement. When people are always told that what they do is awesome (but they are anything but), nobody really believes it when real gifting is affirmed.

One day, the hapless Florence found out the truth. Following the Carnegie Hall event, the New York Sun critic was scathing, declaring that Florence 'could sing everything except notes'. Florence was devastated, suffered a heart attack five days later, and died within a month. Who knows? Perhaps if someone had loved her enough to tell her the truth, she might have a lived a little longer, and a lot happier too.

Faithful are the wounds of a friend, says the wise man in Proverbs. So if you really love someone, and you've earned the right to say what might be uncomfortable to hear but is life-giving in the long term, then for God's sake and theirs, speak tenderly, but speak up. And if you find yourself on the receiving end of advice you don't want to hear, remember that wounds hurt even when they're inflicted by the faithful – but when the initial sting subsides, you'll be glad that they loved you enough to tell you the truth.

I wish I'd known...
THAT GOD CALLS US TO RESPOND TO HIM

In America, it's called 'the altar call'. British evangelicals tend to call it 'the appeal' or 'the response time'. Billy Graham tagged it 'the invitation'. It comes immediately after the sermon, and is an opportunity to make an open response to whatever truth has been preached (especially when the message has an evangelistic flavour). Typically, you are invited to do something: to go public, engage your will, and make an open pledge. The preacher might invite you to raise your hand, signalling commitment, or there might be a more demanding call to walk to the front and join a gathering throng of fellow responders. An eager ministry team are often found waiting in the wings, keen to get their hands on you (sorry, *lay* hands on you) prayerfully. The responding gaggle might even be encouraged to shuffle away to a prepared prayer area, where more intensive ministry can be shared.

Generally, these invitations are positive. Listening to preaching is not something we Christians should do just for entertainment, or to equip us with biblical information that will grant us victory in Bible trivia quizzes. A challenge to make good choices is a good thing. But of course, like everything that we humans put our fallen, sticky fingers on, things can go wrong.

Sometimes the response time seems to be more about validating the preacher than helping the hearers of the message – and I say this as a preacher myself. The odds of this increase when the speaker is labouring under a tonnage of unrealistic expectations. I've preached at a few events where it's clear that the organisers hope that my 30-minute talk will cause thousands to convert (despite there only being a congregation of 47), together with a smattering of mighty healing miracles. Better still would be the resurrecting of a corpse, which will forsake its coffin to live a purpose-driven life. Pressure indeed, especially if only the living are present.

Frantic for a result, the unfortunate preacher feels quite wretched when nobody responds to an impassioned appeal for folks to volunteer as pioneer missionaries who will go to lands where people snack on people. Gradually, the preacher lowers the bar, finally inviting anyone who has recently eaten breakfast to come forward for prayer. Preachers fear the sullen cloud of disappointment that hangs in the air when an event has produced no 'results'.

And then another worrying trend is the 'bait and switch' invitation, where responders are first invited to raise their hand, a prayer is said, but then the hapless hand-raisers are commanded to march up to the front to seal the deal with the aforementioned ministry team.

Sometimes, pressure is placed on others to respond. Parents hope that their phone-clutching 16-year-old tearaway, a diligent student of Facebook throughout the sermon, will tearfully respond at the conclusion of the talk. When the world was rightly shocked by United Airline's less-than-gentle removal of a doctor from an oversold flight, one chap commented that he didn't know what all the fuss was about. Raised as an evangelical, he'd been dragged down the aisle every Sunday morning for years.

But all this said, let's affirm that following Jesus is not just about gathering more information about Him. In a sense, Jesus gave appeals and invited responses. But His calls were often very demanding. A somewhat verbose fisherman called Peter was summoned to follow Him, and even sign up for a life that would lead to a martyr's death. A loaded leader (commonly known as the rich young ruler) heard a call to sell all he had, such was his love affair with stuff (and he decided it was too much for him to do so). And sometimes people made their own responses, like Zacchaeus (who is obviously one of my favourite Bible characters, because he's popped up a few times in this book). Apparently unprompted, except by the beauty of a lunch shared with Jesus, he made costly choices about the corrupt goldmine that was his tax-gathering business.

So if we're in a season of sensing a persistent nudge from God, a whisper of love that invites us to step out or step up, let's take Mary's advice, given when Jesus went as an invited guest to a wedding at Cana where they ran out of wine: 'Do whatever he tells you' (John 2:5). A guest on that occasion, Jesus also gives out invitations, and they carry a standard message with them: RSVP.

Respond, if you please.

I wish I'd known...

THAT SOMETIMES, WE CHRISTIANS NEED TO JUST DO NOTHING

It was obvious to all that my sermon was drawing to a close. Not only had I uttered the words much beloved by congregations everywhere ('and finally...'), but in summarising my key points, it was clear that I was preparing to land the proverbial plane. This was further confirmed by some members of the worship team ambling back on stage, with a keyboard player poised to tickle the keys – final confirmation that this preacher was just about done. But it was then that I sensed heightening tension, because everyone knew what was coming: the time of response. My friends in the Salvation Army have their 'mourner's bench', while Pentecostals in America often provide tissues for the convenience of the tearfully repentant. My listeners braced themselves for the response time. What followed was a surprise to all, including me.

These response times are usually designed to seal the deal, as it were, at the end of the sermon. I've just talked about these 'RSVP' moments, which proves that I either think that they are important, or I spend too much time in church gatherings (and need to get out more), or both. The sermon lays down a challenge: the response time is the moment when the listeners pick up that metaphorical gauntlet, engage their will, and decide. The actual choice varies: it may be a step towards giving more financially, or just giving something. It might be that the respondent is deciding to become a Christian, or determining to pass the good news around more intentionally; they might be turning their back on a destructive pathway currently being trod; they might be making a heart-choice to mend a broken relationship. The idea is simple: *Here's what God says... what are we going to do about it?* Response takes faith from cherished Sunday morning theory to Monday morning action.

And these moments of response can be very, very good. My own father – hardened by the bitterness that had encrusted him during his five years as a half-starved prisoner of war – walked to the front of a church at the conclusion of a Sunday morning service because he decided to follow Christ. It was wonderful, but a little bewildering too, as he walked forward without there being an actual invitation given. The pastor was sharing the end-of-the-service announcements, otherwise known as the notices, so the mildly confused congregation couldn't figure out if Dad was coming home to Jesus, or registering an interest in the ladies embroidery group that meets on Tuesday mornings. It was a beautiful day. That evening, I was preaching in another church, and my parents sat up in the balcony. During my sermon, I pointed up to my dad and said, 'See that man there? He's my father, visiting here all the way from England. This morning he made a response to Jesus, and tonight, he's a Christian.' A thousand people got up and gave him a standing ovation, celebrating his response. He smiled and waved like the Queen.

Whatever the reason for the response, the opportunity to decide is *good*. But all that said, it can get a little tiring. If you've been around Christian subculture for a while, you can start to feel worn out by the responses, especially if you're in a church where an RSVP is extended every Sunday. We can feel overwhelmed by the continual barrage of *coulds*, *shoulds*, *oughts* and *musts*. I'm not suggesting that passive Christianity is the way forward. The Church showcased in the New Testament, while not perfect, was certainly hardworking. They spent their lives and gave their all for the gospel. But that same New Testament talks about the sense of rest that is the heritage of every believer. Belief without effort is meaningless. Belief that is just about effort is exhausting.

Derek Tidball is an esteemed retired college principal, theologian, author and speaker. I was once conducting a radio interview with Derek about his recent book, and I asked him if he could distill all of that learning and reflection into one key statement that he felt was of greatest significance. His answer was this: 'We spend too much time talking about what we can do for God, not enough time talking about what God has done for us in Christ, and when we do talk about what God has done, we then too quickly rush to speak about what we can therefore do for Him.'

In that insightful sentence, Derek handed me a valuable key. In my own life and certainly in the lives of other Christians, I've noticed a sense of fidgety agitation – we never seem to be able to pray enough, give enough, serve enough. The Christian life seems filled with imperatives, calls to action. Discipleship *is* a call to action, but it's a call centred around the finished work of Jesus that leads to peace, the Holy Spirit who empowers us, and partnership with God in what He wants to do *through* us, not just lots of things that we attempt for Him. Today, let's know we're not called to a treadmill, but rather to a 'rest' – resting in God's work, His forgiveness, acceptance, and love that we could never earn.

And so I offered the invitation: 'Tonight, I want you to respond by doing this... Please do absolutely nothing, except... just sit down.

That's right. If you're weary, worn out, disappointed, just do this. Sit down. Don't come forward. Don't pray, or feel compelled to make any decisions. Don't do anything, except take the weight off your feet.'

The result was unexpected. Some hesitated, nervous that a Christian gathering could conclude without the anticipated barrage of imperatives. Some people burst into tears as they just took their seats. Others said that they palpably sensed the presence of God in that moment. Perhaps it was just the relief; the knowledge that being a Christian is not just about what we do for God, but includes resting in all that God has done for us. And after the service was over, numbers of people came up to say how significant the opportunity to just do nothing had been for them.

They simply sat down.

What is Jesus doing right now? One biblical picture has Him sitting down, at the place of final accomplishment and ultimate comfort, at the right hand of the Father. So today, if you are busy for God, thank you for your tireless faithfulness. Sincerely.

And if you're hassled, frazzled, worn out and weary, take five minutes to just be with that seated Jesus... and join Him. Go on. Take the weight off.

Sit down.

I wish I'd known...
THAT 'HOLY' PEOPLE CAN BE THOUGHTLESS PEOPLE

The restaurant was a welcome oasis; we sat down at the outside table with a sigh of relief. Jerusalem's Suk – the bazaar – was a bustling mass of humanity. Shoppers scurried around like ants, hunting for a bargain, some of them uselessly haggling about items that cost less than a pound. Street traders hurried through the labyrinth of cobbled streets, huge trays of fresh bread and bagels impossibly balanced atop their heads. The exotic smell of spices hung fragrant in the air.

But there was an added element to the atmosphere – it was that of religion. A wailing summons to worship blared out from a loud hailer speaker atop a mosque, an insistent cry to the faithful. And as a group of Christian pilgrims, we had found inspiration in seeing the old, old story come to life. I'm not one of those people thrilled to know that Moses had a cappuccino *right here on this very spot* – nevertheless, we had been moved by the old olive trees in the Garden of Gethsemane, their twisted limbs a prophetic picture of the agony and struggle that Jesus experienced there. Galilee's rural simplicity had been a tonic, and the beach at Tabgha is always a joy. It was there that Jesus cooked breakfast for His weary friends

– an unusual act after beating the powers of death and hell in His resurrection, but a beautiful example of His relentless care.

We were hungry for our lunch, and a smiling waiter had welcomed us and offered menus. Suddenly, a group of Christians plonked themselves down at the table next to us. Their t-shirts loudly announced that they were believers: 'I follow a Jewish carpenter', said one. Another had 'Faithbook. Add Jesus as a friend', which either suggested that the wearer was (a) into social media or (b) wrestling with a lisp (or both). Incredibly, a third proclaimed that 'The world is a battlefield. God is my weapon. The Bible is my ammo'. What? God is a weapon? The Bible is ammo? Ammunition is used to kill people. Apparently, this group had all shopped at www.hideousreligioustshirts.com for their attire.

But their fashion choices were just the beginning of sorrows. Seemingly oblivious to the fact that sitting in a food establishment usually means ordering from the menu, they opened their bags and tucked into their sandwiches that they'd brought with them. One of them even produced a thermos flask with hot drinks. And of course, no eating began before a lengthy prayer of grace was shared, asking the Lord to bless the food. The restaurant owner was probably not greatly blessed himself, but smiled patiently. I wondered how many times he, an orthodox Jew, spotted pilgrims behaving badly. I shot him a look, but there was no hint of frustration. This must be a regular event that he'd grown used to: Christians behaving badly.

Something similar happened when Kay and I attended a large national prayer event recently. A huge queue of people lined up patiently to get in. The presence of the President of the United States meant that security was high, and creating a secure environment takes time. Suddenly, a leader and his entourage rudely pushed their way to the front. I informed the queue-jumpers that they should take their place at the back of the line. 'That's where we were just now,' one of them glowered, somewhat menacingly, 'and now we're here.' And there they stood, bustling for first place – into a *prayer meeting*. I contemplated further action, but a punch-up prior to a period of intercession would be quite unseemly. The incongruity of pushing in to pray apparently didn't occur. Christians behaving badly.

Jesus warns us against allowing a dab of piety to blind us to obvious realities. Being picky about gnats but swallowing camels whole is a dangerous tendency among those who are spiritually keen. The Pharisees were white-hot on rules for eating, but equally fervent about whipping up a conspiracy to condemn an innocent man to death. Faith should bring focus to our lives, offering a faithful reflection in a mirror-mirror-on-the-wall, who's-the-fairest-of-them-all culture. But sometimes a bit of religious devotion can blind us to the reality of us. We ignore what is obviously wrong in our lives, justifying ourselves by what is 'right' in our lives. Able to spot the faults of others from a great distance, we're keen to help them remove the tiniest specks from their eyes, while ignoring the great logs that protrude from our own.

I recently chatted with a man whose work ethic is shocking. (If there was a Guinness World Record for low productivity and taking time off, he'd win by a country mile.) He spent most of our conversation complaining about his boss who, he says, is lazy and unproductive. There's that log again.

So asking God to show us what we don't currently see about ourselves is surely a healthy prayer to pray.

And this is vital. Some people don't become followers of Jesus because they don't know any Christians. And some people don't turn to Christ precisely because they *do* know some of His crowd.

Their meal over, the t-shirted snackers moved on, eager for the next epiphany. I hope they didn't leave their paper bags and soiled cups behind for the server to clear away. But who knows? Perhaps they did. After all, they were in a restaurant.

I wish I'd known...
THAT THE GIFT OF DISILLUSIONMENT IS PRICELESS

It was a stormy day in Colorado. I looked out across the foothills of the Rockies towards the monumental Longs Peak, a snow-capped mountain that rises 14,000 feet. And, in a phenomenon that I have only noticed in the Western USA, I could see bands of rain coming our way. Five or six minutes later, we would be drenched. But at that moment, the rainfall was still a mile away, though edging relentlessly towards us.

This is how I used to view disillusionment. As an idealist but a realist too, I knew that the raincloud of disillusionment was out there. Sooner or later, it would overwhelm me, blotting out the sunshine of hope. Worse still, I knew that disillusionment usually distills into cynicism.

And through the years, I've tried to swat those clouds away. I've been disillusioned with friends; people I thought would be lifelong companions on the journey marched or drifted away. Some people that I thought were at least positive acquaintances turned nasty when they reached a place of power.

Church has been a major source of disillusionment. Denominational leaders that I revered played political games, set colleagues up for downfall, and lied while all the time declaring that truth matters.

When I became part of the so-called new church movement (charismatic house churches that were birthed in the UK in the 1970s), there was a heady sense among us that we were going to change the world by next Tuesday. If disillusionment sometimes distills into cynicism, then optimism can morph into arrogance – some of us thought we were the answer to the planet. Some major initiatives did emerge from our efforts (in fact, the worldwide 24-7 Prayer movement, spearheaded by the tremendous leadership of Pete Grieg, was birthed out of our church). But our heady hopes were not all realised. Disillusioning.

And I've been disillusioned with myself. I thought that, over 40 years on from that day when I decided to follow Jesus, I would understand more, pray more effectively, and generally be a much more mature human being now. No longer would I be ruffled by drivers who drive too fast ('Idiots…'), drive too slow ('Get out of my way, *now*…'), and I would be impervious to the minor irritations that everyday church life creates ('If we sing that song one more time, I'm going to physically attack the worship leader…'). At times, I have surprised myself with the things that I've said and done, and not in a positive way. I'm disappointed; disillusioned with *me*.

But recently I've been learning that we shouldn't fear disillusionment – instead, let's choose to welcome it as a priceless gift. Put simply, disillusionment divests us of an illusion. The process itself is usually painful – often we cling to a mythical view of life, cherishing it and reluctant to part with it, because we prefer it to the reality, so abandoning it brings grief. But ultimately, disillusionment takes us by the hand and leads us, albeit reluctantly, to a place of reality rather than romanticism.

We were born into an illusionary world, one in which we are the centre of the universe. If you're hungry, just yell. Someone will come running with food. There's no need to look for a toilet: just poo, wherever you are, whenever you like. (It works when you're a month old; don't try it at 25.) Maturity dispels illusion and gradually introduces us to the way the world really works. The illusion fades: we are not the centre of everything.

Jesus spent much of His time in a ministry of disillusionment – and not just among the Pharisees, who were saddened because He refused to dance to their religious tune. And His disciples needed the ministry of disillusionment too. As good Jewish boys, they had a defined expectation of a Messiah figure. He would surely go to Jerusalem, kick out those oppressive Romans, and set up an earthly throne there, from which He would reign over a new theocratic Israel. That's why James and John went to Jesus (hiding behind their mother, Salome) with a request for thrones at His side. They had their sights firmly set on political and social power in the limited time/space world that was Israel. But they needed to be disillusioned. And it was so difficult to prise that dream from their hearts and minds, so deeply embedded was it in Israel's national psyche.

Some of the disciples were taken to a place of disillusionment about themselves, too. Peter, for example, was living under the total illusion that he would never be unfaithful to Jesus; even if all his pals succumbed to pressure, he would stand firm. But Jesus shattered that illusion with news that included a rooster crowing three times.

When I allow disillusionment to enter my friendships, I'm no longer shattered when someone close to me fails to listen, or switches the conversation back onto themselves when I'm trying to pour out my heart. Similarly, disillusionment is vital for a healthy marriage, because real life is just so unlike the movies. In those romantic comedies, nobody snores, drools on the pillow, or struggles unsuccessfully with flatulence in the middle of the night. And after a blissful night of love, they greet each other in the morning with a lengthy kiss in a make-believe world where morning breath (that could knock you off your feet at 20 yards) doesn't exist. But in reality, though the mythical notions of the honeymoon fade over the years, they are replaced by something far more substantial – real love for a real person, rather than infatuation with what we hope a perfect person might be like.

And disillusionment is very important if we're going to spend any length of time in a local church. When we join, we anticipate that the music will be to our liking, the sermon always relevant, and the people in our small group interesting, kind and supportive. And then we find that the place is littered with fragile, thoughtless, in-the-process human beings just like us... and the illusion is shattered. Now we have a choice. Will we move on to the next church (usually justifying our move by saying that the Lord is telling us to go), or will we stick around, grit our teeth, and learn something about real commitment?

Setting out on a recent holiday, I packed disillusionment and took it along with me together with some lightweight novels and sun cream. It helped me no end, because I've tended to believe that everything will be perfect when I set time aside for a break. The sun will shine, the hotel will be exactly as portrayed in the brochure, and there will be no roving Europeans hogging the sunbeds. When our holiday includes wider family or friends, everyone will get along together wonderfully, there will be no tension about what we do each day, every restaurant we visit will be to everyone's liking and we will happily toast the sunset together at the end of yet another glorious day. But it's an illusion. So when the junior members of our 'happy' band fight like cats and it rains all day and the place we choose to eat at is nothing less than appalling, I'm not surprised. I'm not jaundiced or cynical – just realistic with my expectations.

Finally, I'm completely disillusioned with me, and it's been a lifesaver. It's not that I don't have high expectations of myself – I do. I like to behave like a Christian, behave like a good husband, father and grandfather, and be faithful and attentive in my friendships. But my expectations are balanced by low expectations. When other leaders lash up their lives with scandalous moral choices, I no longer wrinkle my nose and insist that I could *never* walk the sinful path they have trodden. Rather, I acknowledge my capacity for sin, and manage vulnerability instead of insisting that I'm impervious to temptation. I don't want to hear that rooster crowing.

And so I no longer fear disillusionment. Instead I embrace it, lest I, a broken person, walk around a broken planet surrounded by broken people – with my eyes wide shut.

Disillusionment. It probably hasn't appeared on your 'most desired gift' list. But perhaps it should.

I wish I'd known...
THAT THE INEVITABLE IS NOT INEVITABLE

The visiting preacher, having called all those who wanted prayer for healing to make their way to the front, was being just a little too enthusiastic for my liking. Rushing up and down with a bottle of anointing oil in his hands, he paused briefly with each one, but spent noticeably longer with those who had less challenging maladies. The people using wheelchairs were given just a brief moment, but those with minor aches and pains seemed to get a lot of attention. The chap with a stiff arm was told to wave it about after prayer, and when he did so and claimed that there was no pain, the congregation clapped and cheered. Call me cynical if you like, but I believe that leaders are required to exercise healthy scepticism when large claims are made. The preacher, thrilled to get a glimmer of a result, yelled breathlessly into the microphone, 'That's it! You're healed!'... I wasn't so sure.

But this much I knew for certain: while the preacher was leaving town tomorrow, as a local leader, I had to stay behind, and perhaps clear up the damage done either by hurried claims of healing, or to those who had been stirred to false hope but for whom nothing had actually happened.

Now please don't misunderstand. I believe that God still heals today. It's just that four decades of ministry, most of it based in local churches, has shown me that genuine, authenticated healing doesn't happen as often as we'd like, or as often as is claimed. And that reality has caused me to groan when news of a serious or terminal illness breaks in a local congregation. Rightly stirred into prayerful action, everyone goes into furious intercessory mode, calling upon the Lord for a miracle. The fact that the miracle rarely arrives has caused me to almost unconsciously drift into an attitude of accepting inevitability as inevitable. When the grim-faced doctor proffers that terrible diagnosis, I tend to believe that it's going to go the way that he or she suggests, however much we pray.

But then I re-read one of my favourite stories in the Bible, and am challenged to think and believe for the impossible once more. It's the account of jailed Peter being supernaturally set free as a result of the church's prayers (Acts 12:1–19). As far as tough situations go, it's right up there, and Luke, in sharing what happened, wants us to know just how impossible Peter's situation was. The ex-fisherman was being held in a maximum security situation, presumably because the authorities had heard that God had previously broken His servants out of jail. Herod, the puppet-king who had ordered the arrest, meant serious business – James had already been beheaded. Peter had been temporarily spared by a calendar formality (executions were not permitted during Passover), so Herod was just waiting a few days before putting the Church's leading spokesman to the sword. Not only was Peter on death row, but he was being watched by four squads of four soldiers each. Everything looked utterly hopeless. It was surely time to plan a funeral, because Peter's death looked inevitable.

And there was another reason for the church to be tempted to think that nothing could be done. Instead of praying, they could have decided that, seeing as Peter dying a martyr's death was clearly predicted by Jesus, this was the fulfillment of that prophecy, and so there was nothing to be done, no prayers to be prayed.

Jesus had predicted trouble ahead for both Peter and James. When James' mother Salome had asked Jesus to allocate thrones for her sons, Jesus solemnly warned them that the cup of suffering was ahead for them both. That promise had tragically been fulfilled now, as James was executed at Herod's command. Peter, similarly, had been told that he would die a martyr's death, during the lakeside breakfast that Jesus shared with His friends after the resurrection. And now martyrdom seemed certain. Within hours, Peter would surely suffer the same fate. The Church could have shrugged their shoulders, comforted each other that at least this was something that Jesus had clearly foreseen, and accepted the tragedy as God's will. But they didn't. Their discerning hearts urged them to continue in prayer.

But even in that praying, they wrestled with the thought that they were offering a request that could never be answered. Put simply, they expected Peter to die even as they asked. Their response when he eventually shows up after an angelic jailbreak makes that plain.

Meanwhile, back at the jail, an angel wakes Peter up, and has to give careful commands about him getting dressed, because Peter thinks he's dreaming. Once out of the prison, still-sleepy Peter heads for the place where the church is gathered, and a comedic scene unfolds. So busy praying that they didn't want to break off to open the door, Rhoda, a servant girl, is sent to answer the knocking. (That action is a little strange – the Church is in the midst of terrifying persecution, and the knock at the door could have come from soldiers sent to carry out yet more arrests, but a lone woman is sent to open it...)

Rhoda is stunned – but also filled with joy – when she discovers who's there, so much so that she rushes back into the prayer meeting without opening the door! Rhoda breathlessly shares that Peter is outside, but her claim is met with dismissive incredulity. This gaggle of faithful Christians who are praying for Peter think she must be out of her mind, and tell her so. What she is saying seems so ridiculous that they dismiss her report as a far-fetched, even insane notion.

What God had done was beyond the realm of their thinking. A popular idea among the Jews at the time was the belief that the spirit or 'ghost' of a person lingered for a few days after their death. That's why the praying faithful thought that this is what Rhoda had seen – and that's most likely why Jesus took such pains to prove that He still had a physical body when He appeared to His disciples (His was very definitely a physical bodily resurrection). So why were those at the prayer gathering convinced that Peter must surely be dead?

For one thing, James *was* dead. When our hopes have been disappointed in the past, we're more reluctant to continue in expectation as a result. The bruises and scars of difficulty and tragedy can rob us of faith for the present. And then surely this group was fearful too. If James was dead and Peter was also gone, who would be next? Fear limits God, which is one reason why I fear fear. Fear says that God might be able to do only so much, but surely not that which is beyond reason.

So, jumping back into the story, Peter is still outside. (It took an angel to get Peter out of prison, but once the angel left his side, he couldn't get into the prayer meeting! One door opened 'all by itself' and the other slammed back in his face.) He is still effectively on the run from death row, is unsafe, and vulnerable to being picked up and arrested by any passing Roman soldier. But he keeps on knocking, and his patience is finally rewarded. At last he walks into a prayer gathering being held with the sole purpose of petitioning God for his release – only to be met with a stunned response.

We can go through moments and seasons when faith seems absurd, even mad. When we hear of yet another senseless atrocity, or when that faithful Christian meets a horrible end, while an evil despot prospers, there seems no rhyme or reason to the universe, and we edge to the awful thought: what if there is no God at the heart of everything? When Christians have these thoughts, they can feel like doubting traitors – how can they really be saved if these ideas circle their minds? This praying group were right in the middle of a miracle, all while thinking that claiming divine intervention like this was just mad.

Faith is not a consistent walk, but sometimes an uphill trek, and doubt is a normal part of it for most. So if trusting feels crazy, don't heap condemnation on yourself and makes matters worse. Whatever you feel, may God help you and me to trust Him anyway.

Not only is what is difficult possible, but the impossible is possible too. Lately, I've revived prayers for seemingly impossible situations in my own life, prayers that I had neglected because, frankly, I'd given up. But I've started asking again, because with God all things are possible. We don't see miracles as much as we'd like. But that should not prevent us from realising that they are possible, and that we are still called to pray.

Disappointed? Pray again. Fearful? Pray again. And then some.

At the beginning of this episode, Herod is the power broker, the one who holds all the cards in his hand. But by the end, he is the weak, feeble person who dies as a result of the judgment of God – Luke's description of Herod as being eaten by worms is probably related to the abdominal pains referred to in an account from Josephus, the Jewish historian. But in contrast with Herod's demise is this statement: 'But the word of the Lord spread' (one of Luke's favourite terms – he uses it twice elsewhere in Acts). Luke wants us to know that the demagogue falls. The cell door opens. The Roman security system fails. The praying church, even in the midst of its doubting, triumphs.

But there's one other element to this story that we shouldn't miss: even when the inevitable is thwarted and a miracle comes, that doesn't resolve all questions. As the gathered church finally realised that their prayers had actually been answered, spare a thought for Salome, the mother of James, who had been executed. The question that must have tormented her was this: if God could release Peter, why wasn't her beloved boy spared? While everybody else was celebrating, perhaps she was quietly weeping in a corner, trying to come to terms with her own grief while Peter was receiving congratulatory slaps on the back.

It's often been said that unanswered prayer creates questions and conflict, but the truth is that *answered* prayer creates its own issues. In our local church now, we are dealing with a tragedy where some were wonderfully spared in a horrible road accident, while two other much-loved members of our church family were killed. And every testimony of healing has the same effect, not only on those who continue to suffer with long-term illness, but upon those who love them and have to witness their suffering: why was one prayer answered, and another not?

When miracles happen, let's not hide them, but give thanks to the God who performed them. But let's also be caring and sensitive towards those who continue to wait and wonder, lest we hurt them with our joy. It's called rejoicing with those who rejoice, and weeping with those who weep.

I wish I'd known...
THAT GOSSIP IS DELICIOUS, BUT DEADLY

It was an odd conversation about another Christian leader, who had just been promoted to a position of national leadership. A fellow minister was raising some concerns about this man's suitability for the position, but had no specific, tangible evidence for his hesitation: 'I'm not sure what it is about him,' he mused. 'It's just, when he stands up to speak, although his preaching is fine, there's just something... I can't put my finger on it... something that's not quite right about him. It's a strong feeling that I have. I think there's a skeleton in that cupboard.' And then, to endorse his unspecified suspicion, the minister added, 'And I'm not the only one who feels this way. There are a number of people around the country who believe the same thing. Something is going to emerge, I'm sure of it.'

Brilliant. The newly-promoted leader's character had been smeared, and all on the basis of a vague feeling. There was no evidence of anything being wrong, but suspicion had been raised – and passed around – simply because of a hunch. And for all I know, that hunch might have been created by jealousy, or perhaps an altercation in the past that had never been resolved. Christians have ingenious ways to hurt each other.

Scripture tells us to be careful about bringing accusations about those in leadership, but surely that unwillingness to engage in sullying another person's character should apply to all people. Let's not create suspicion with vague, spiritual nonsense. It's called gossip.

Gossip is as tempting as a Sunday roast. Scripture tells us that, 'The words of a gossip are like choice morsels; they go down to the inmost parts' (Prov. 18:8). Perhaps that's why rumour-mongering and negative whispering are such a problem in churches (and wherever human beings gather). There's such a perverse delight in hearing and sharing gossip. Just as we thoroughly enjoy and relish every single bite of an exquisitely prepared and expensive meal, so gossiping is a rather delicious experience. Suddenly the person whose gifts and talents intimidate us is cut down to size, and we feel better about our own inadequacies; our hunger for scandal is satisfied. We are perceived as someone who is in the know, because we are privy to this inside information. Knowledge is a sign of power, and in passing on the rumour, we feel powerful. And in sharing gossip, there's always the possibility that the conversation will unearth yet more negative news. All of this allows us to hurt someone we dislike, fear, are irritated or intimidated by, without ever having to strike a physical blow. Proverbs tells us that words can be like three terrible weapons – a battle-axe, a sword, and an arrow. That's an impressive and potentially devastating arsenal.

Gossip is junk food. It leaves a lingering aftertaste, because we know we have been unjust and cowardly in our whispering. So, when tempted to gossip – and the moment comes to us all – please step away from that morsel. It will upset your stomach, and wound someone else's heart.

I wish I'd known...
THAT GOD IS OPEN TO SUGGESTIONS

Vision. It's what all churches need. And for most of my ministry, I assumed that vision was something generated by God, passed on to leaders by the Holy Spirit, and then shared by a local congregation. Top-down instructions. Commands from God to be followed. A strategy to be obeyed. And when I look at the Early Church, there are clear instances of that. After just one year of nurturing the new congregation in Antioch, Saul (later known as Paul) is the subject of a clear directive from God: set apart Barnabas and Saul for the task I've appointed them. And a stunning team is birthed following that command. Multitudes are converted, healthy churches planted. Of course, even when God Himself issues a command, there's no guarantee that human fragility won't mess things up, as the permanent spat that split the Paul/Barnabas team tragically demonstrates.

But there are other instances of top-down vision. A sheet full of unclean animals in Peter's rooftop vision, signalling the open door for the Gentiles into the Church. A 'man from Macedonia' summoning Paul to come over and help with the gospel. God in the driving seat. Do this. Go there.

But then there are times when it seems that God is open to suggestions. As we've seen, Peter's famous walk on the turbulent waters of the Sea of Galilee began not with Jesus coming up with the idea, but Peter suggesting it. Granted, he waited for Jesus' approval of the notion: 'Lord, if it's you, let me come to you'. But it was still Peter's idea, albeit one that Jesus agreed to.

An even more radical example is found at the beginning of Jesus' ministry, when the wedding wine ran out, which was more than a minor problem. Not providing adequate hospitality for one's guests would have brought lasting shame on the families of the bride and groom, and would not have just ruined their day, but would have cast a shadow over their reputations for years to come. Jesus' mother, Mary, was known to be pushy at times (she once tried to organise a family intervention and forcibly take Jesus back to His home village when she was concerned about His mental health). She suggests a solution: let Jesus take care of it. But in this case, Jesus objected, insisting that the time for these things was not yet at hand. However, when she insisted, He conceded. The first miracle of His ministry was not just someone else's idea, it resulted from parental pressure.

But then not every idea presented to Jesus was met with His approval. James and John discovered that when they angrily wanted to annihilate a Samaritan village. Peter also found himself on the receiving end of a stinging rebuke when suggesting that, for Jesus, the cross was not a good idea. Other initiatives received the thumbs-down, like dismissing the parents of the children that were brought to Jesus for blessing, or rebuking a woman who gave an extravagant gift of perfume to Jesus – an outrageous act of generosity that was worth a year's wages. When the disciples wrinkled their noses and made somewhat hollow speeches about the poor, Jesus silenced their objections (and their verbal attack on the woman) without hesitation. So not every idea was adopted.

That said, let's realise that God is open to suggestions – even if, at times, this calls for Him to change His mind. Abraham discovered that in a lengthy session of negotiation with God. Trying to make a deal for Sodom and Gomorrah, Abraham succeeded in nudging the Lord to relent. Theologians and commentators choke at this. But what is prayer if it does not include the offering of suggestions to God, as we present our requests?

And so very soon, at Timberline Church, we are going to have a 'dreaming' session. We'll invite a number of our leaders to give five-minute 'Ted'-type talks where they can share their wildest dreams, not just for their departments, but for the whole church. And then we'll gather up our armfuls of dreams, and offer them to Jesus, whose church it is. Who knows which of our suggestions He might agree to?

So be bold in prayer. Make suggestions in faith, and be faithful if they're not heeded. As we acknowledge that God is truly open to suggestions, we discover that this partnership between Him and us is perhaps more substantial – and is loaded with more potential – than we ever imagined.

I wish I'd known...

THAT SOMETIMES IT TAKES FAITH TO STAY AS WELL AS GO

I've been there. It's a rocky hillside that used to slope down all the way to the Sea of Galilee. The water is much lower these days and so the slope stops several hundred metres short of the shoreline, so a little imagination is needed. But the story of the Gadarene demoniac encountering Jesus is told with such detail and vivid colour, it's easy to stand there and picture the harrowing scene. Jesus is confronted by a screaming madman, a pitiful creature tormented by multiple demons. It's terrifying, so much so that it could easily be a product of Stephen King's imagination. There's despair, agony, violence, and the intimidating power of devilish control, all of which are dominating this poor man's life. But when Jesus comes by, everything is different. No matter how dark the situation, how ingrained destructive patterns are in someone's life, Jesus can turn things around. And the previously tormented man has a new agenda.

When we meet Jesus, our world-view changes. The Spirit of God generates change in us that is more than external behavioural revision: the same power that raised Christ from the dead is working in us, shaping and forming us into what God intends.

If we insist that we have met and are meeting with God in a faith walk, but there's been little change made in our lives, let's question whether we are experiencing the real deal. Jesus doesn't just bring comfort, but challenge and revolution. There's always a danger that we settle for a nominal imitation of faith, a dab of God, if you will, for Sunday mornings, but nothing that would make much difference to the way we do Monday mornings.

Faith can become a token, a vague add-on rather than the core of who were are. Wilbur Rees describes that kind of nominalism in his famous poem:

'I would like to buy $3 worth of God, please.
Not enough to explode my soul or disturb my sleep,
but just enough to equal a cup of warm milk
or a snooze in the sunshine.
I don't want enough of God to make me love a black man
or pick beets with a migrant.
I want ecstasy, not transformation.
I want warmth of the womb, not a new birth.
I want a pound of the Eternal in a paper sack.
I would like to buy $3 worth of God, please.'

But the former demoniac from Gadera experiences far more than a manageable portion of God. The screaming voices in his head are silenced at last. The relentless desire to harm himself is banished, to be replaced by a peace that is thick, but mysterious. Little wonder his first thought is to join Jesus' team.

Thrilled beyond belief at his own deliverance, the formerly tormented man asks if he can accompany Jesus. Stop for a moment. Think how useful the shared testimony of such a man might be.

He had terrorised a community with his evil outbursts, and was now fully in his right mind, delivered and restored. But his offering of himself to travel with Jesus and His team is refused – he has another mission to attend to, one that involves his own people. He is called not to go, but to stay.

When we think of others making big faith steps, travelling to different locations and embracing change happily, we can fret, wondering if our faith is worth much. But there are times when it takes more faith to stay than it takes to go, when faith calls us not to flee but to stand our ground. It's ordinary, and possibly nowhere near as exciting. But if that's what God says to you, then do it.

What matters is not the staying or the going, but the walking with Jesus, wherever the location, today. Radical conversion is not measured by the distance subsequently travelled or the upheaval experienced, but by the faithfulness offered. If you're called to stay, then embrace the adventure that is offered to those who obediently remain.

I wish I'd known...
THAT IT'S A GOOD IDEA TO LEAVE EARLY

It sounds so very obvious, but over the years, I wish I'd left early – be it for travel, appointments, the airport or the dentist (OK, not the dentist). Rushing is what I tend to spend my life doing. And it's mainly because of one simple, debilitating habit: I like to calculate how much time it will take me to get somewhere, and then leave with exactly that amount to complete the journey. This means that I am constantly clock-watching while getting to meetings at my church office (28 minutes and 30 seconds away if traffic is light and the one traffic light that I despise is kind enough to be green).

This habit means that I feel frantic as I dash to the airport (one hour 14 minutes if I don't go through the drive-through place on the way for a coffee), hoping and praying that I'll be there on time, feeling massively stressed throughout the journey and arriving somewhat emotionally fractured. Ironically, in trying to achieve more, I achieve less, because my head is brimming with anxiety and I waste the journey time; instead of reflecting or planning, I'm too busy worrying that I'm going to miss that plane.

I have also sprinted through airports to get to departure gates, and on one occasion many years ago, our plane had actually pulled away onto the runway, but because my last-minute antics had caused two families to be late (that's a lot of empty seats), they actually pulled the aeroplane back to the gate and allowed us on – something that would never happen today. The sound of tut-tutting from the other passengers as our breathless, sweaty group boarded the then delayed plane was understandably deafening.

Ironically, I am a very punctual person and I believe that being late is insulting, because a delay costs other people time. When I am late, not only am I delayed, but I send a message to those that I am meeting that I do not consider their time to be important. It becomes a habit. I know people who were probably late being born, and have been consistently late ever since. If they arrive punctually, then it's a surprise. Now they have a reputation, and one for not keeping their word.

In a way, being late is theft. Horace Mann put it rather bluntly: 'Unfaithfulness in the keeping of an appointment is an act of clear dishonesty. You may as well borrow a person's money as their time.'

Sometimes, being late brings total disaster. Earlier I mentioned the unfortunate fact that Thomas missed that epic meeting with Jesus, which created a week of shadows. Nobody knows what he was doing and why he wasn't there. Perhaps he knew he'd be late for the gathering because of poor planning, so he didn't bother.

But there's another episode in the Bible where we can be certain that a delayed arrival created all kinds of problems. Samuel had agreed to meet nervous King Saul, and he was just a little late. I'm not talking 20 minutes, or even an hour. Saul had been told to wait a *week* for Samuel to arrive, but even then, Samuel missed the deadline, and Saul's demoralised troops began to scatter. Saul panicked and offered sacrifices – a job reserved exclusively for the priesthood. We're not told why Samuel was delayed, but his lateness certainly had dire consequences.

So keep your word. Don't say the cheque is in the post if it isn't. Leave early. And be on time.

I wish I'd known...
THAT WE'RE ALL BROKEN, BUT THERE'S POWER AVAILABLE

I've written about it elsewhere, but since this realisation has been so important to me, I'd like to include it here as I continue to consider things I wish I'd known. Certainly the knowledge of the truth we're pondering today would have saved me from being hurt by disappointment, and spared me from navigating depressing seasons when I was shattered by the inconsistencies of other people, and especially the flaws that are in the Church.

The truth is simply, bluntly this: everything is broken.

Everything. Every person, marriage, organisation, church, business – no matter how together and whole they may seem, there are hairline fractures and deficiencies, because we live in a world that is broken and fallen. As followers of Jesus, we are being perfected, but are not yet perfect. It's a vital truth for us to grasp, because we Christians are visionary people with high hopes, and when those hopes are dashed, we can feel like faith is hollow and pointless.

As I've said, I'm no longer surprised when people make mad decisions and blunder into destructive sin, or when fellow leaders serve God with mixed motives and sometimes clumsy actions. Nobody ever did anything out of 100% pure motives, with the obvious exception of Jesus. Like me, and like you, they are broken, under-construction people. One day, when Christ comes, wholeness will be ours. In the meantime, the realisation that everything is broken is no invitation or licence to sin, but is surely a vital antidote against devastating disappointment.

But this is only half of the truth. Paul tells us that there is treasure in earthen vessels. So though everything is broken, it's not the end of the story. Often, when we think about what goes on inside our heads and hearts, we focus only on the negative, recognising that we are fallen, fragile human beings. Surely that is what we hear from Paul as he confesses that he tends to do what he should not do, and shies away from what is right. His words are so honest and vulnerable that some have concluded that he was talking about his life *before* he found Christ – a conclusion that I disagree with. Having Jesus in your life doesn't end the struggle – the spirit is still willing, and the flesh is still weak. But we're wrong to only think about our inner beings in negative terms. There is another power at work within us too – the power of the Holy Spirit, actively working to help us, to daily shape us into all that God wants us to be in Christ.

I've been surprised by that beautiful impelling. Faced with moments of temptation, I have suddenly found myself desperately wanting to do what is right with such compulsion that it conquered the nudge to do what was wrong. I wondered where that overwhelming surge came from, and concluded that this was more than a rebuke from conscience or simply a hope that I could live by what was morally right – this was true power, power that rescued me from potential disaster.

So everything *is* broken. But in the midst of our brokenness, there is power – resurrection power – to impel us, reconstruct us, and heal us. Thank God for that.

I wish I'd known...
THAT BOTH TRUTH AND TONE MATTER

We live in an age of tolerance. Scratch that: we live in an age where tolerance is the new god, to be revered and worshipped. If you're seen to be intolerant, then you're a bigoted, narrow, arrogant low-life and your contrary opinion is hateful, because there's one thing that we just can't tolerate these days, and that's an opinion that is contrary to the consensus. The thought that the majority might be wrong just doesn't seem to occur, even if we are related to the folks who thought for centuries that the earth was the centre of the universe and that the sun circled it, until in 1534 Copernicus politely pointed out that we are not the centre of everything, but rather are circling the sun.

The Church has failed miserably in this department too. Galileo was another who proved that a herd mentality is not great when it comes to being right about what's what, and his support of Copernicus' ideas led him to clash with the Catholic Church of his day. He was placed under house arrest for his 'heretical' views and was held captive for the rest of his life. Once again, the majority was wrong.

But woe betide the person who breaks step with the consensus, who walks apart from the crowd.

Just recently, a beauty pageant contestant in America was asked her opinion about same-sex marriages. She replied (with gentle graciousness) that she believed that marriage was designed to be a relationship between a man and a woman. The judge who put the question was incensed, she lost the crown, and an international media flurry broke out, including a demand that she apologise for her comment. This is liberal fundamentalism; while insisting that everyone has the right to free speech and free choice, the guns are quickly turned on anyone who dares to disagree; they will feel the heart of fundamentalist ire if they do. Liberal fundamentalism indeed.

Why? She spoke no spiteful words of homophobic hatred, just simply answered the question expressing her own personal convictions in a measured manner. But we are living in a time when some people act like the thought police, insisting that we agree with their views while, as I've said, all the time demanding 'tolerance'. If she had spoken up *for* gay rights and then lost the crown because of it, there would have been an outrage – rightly. As it turned out, her quiet courage opened the door for many media opportunities to speak about her views on human sexuality. Her voice was welcome; it was no rant, but a steady voice. In a world of political correctness gone mad, it can be difficult to hold an opinion that is contrary to the popular trend – whatever the topic or issue. Let's be willing to be unpopular, not for unkindness, but for conviction.

But there's a vital truth that Christians can often miss when we speak up about our values, and one that we can learn from that pageant contestant. It's not only the content of our message that matters; the tone of it is important too. Passionate people can sound strident and aggressive, and there is also a temptation to be angry when we feel that our viewpoint is being suppressed. And when that happens, we can come across as ranting, yelling people who are regarded as suspicious. We are called to persuade, not pummel people with our words. Sometimes the world can't hear a word of what we're saying because they are too put off by the way that we say it.

It was a wonder that Jesus spent so much time in the company of the despised 'sinners' of His day – but an even greater miracle that they wanted to spend time with Him. The holiest person who has ever walked the earth was a sought-after party guest, and the kind of person that children lined up to hug – not usually a problem for wide-eyed fanatical types. His winsome storytelling nudged people to think and discover truth; His preaching didn't involve blasting people with right ideas, but edged them forward to discovery.

So let's be willing to break step and have the courage of our convictions, but be kind as we express them.

I wish I'd known...
THAT AGITATION IS SOMETIMES A GIFT FROM GOD

It's a rather stark confession, but as I travel, I spend much of my time feeling not really at home in the churches I visit, and it has nothing to do with a lack of welcome. It's just that I love the Church – and I can therefore feel very quickly frustrated with her.

I recently spoke at a lovely united church gathering, but the prayer meeting beforehand unnerved me. It seemed that everyone else wanted God to smite His people with guilt and shame. I felt uncomfortable, and somewhat out of place. Even more recently, I spoke in an ultra-charismatic church and felt displaced in the prayer meeting for an entirely different reason. This group (who are highly committed and very effective) equated passion in prayer with volume, and yelled at God to do their bidding. Again, I shifted from one foot to another, feeling displaced and agitated. It's awkward and uncomfortable to feel that sense of disquiet. I'd like to feel at home wherever I am, which is completely unrealistic.

And so I've decided that it's OK to feel agitated, and some of us will have that 'gift' for the rest of our days, especially those of us called to the privilege of serving in a leadership capacity. We long for the Church to be more real, more thoughtful; we ache for a more effective Church, one that can genuinely make an impact in our hurting world. Of course, our longing doesn't mean that we are right. But perhaps the gift of agitation can help fuel our prayers, strengthen our commitment, and galvanise us into service.

Paul felt the pain of being 'burdened' for the churches; Jesus was frustrated at the slowness of His disciples. Perhaps you feel agitated too. Don't let that pain nudge you into arrogance or surrender. If you feel concerned about the Church, or agitated about faith in general, you may need to make friends with agitation. It will likely be with you for the rest of your life.

And it's OK to sometimes feel despair about the way things are. Wherever we got the idea that faith means that we will be endlessly happy, it certainly didn't come from the New Testament. Paul chose being despised over the prestigious position of respect that a Pharisee enjoyed. Peter and his Galilean friends turned their backs on a safe, predictable existence for the precarious pathway of following Jesus. They didn't hop, skip and jump through the three heady years that they spent on the trail with Him. As well as the obvious highlights there were times of doubt, abject confusion, fear, and foolishness all mingled together. But they stayed with it, convinced that the one who described Himself as the way, the truth and the life had it right. Following the right path took priority over always being happy.

As C.S. Lewis put it: 'I didn't go to religion to make me happy. I always knew a bottle of Port would do that. If you want a religion to make you feel really comfortable, I certainly don't recommend Christianity.'[1]

So next time agitation raises its head, shake it by the hand. It might lead you to realise that you're unwilling to settle for what is, and continue to hunger for what might be.

---

[1] C.S. Lewis, *God in the Dock* © Copyright C.S. Lewis Pte Ltd 1970. Used with permission.

I wish I'd known...
THAT SOME CHRISTIAN SLOGANS ARE OUTRIGHT LIES

It's proudly displayed in my office, a 'gift' from a prankster friend who knows how much some Christian clichés and slogans irritate me. It's a plaque purchased from our local Christian bookshop, which declares in capital letters that I should 'dance to the beat of my angel's wings'. (More about that later...) The gift was prompted by a conversation we recently shared where I lambasted some of the statements we routinely make in worship songs, statements that are patently untrue. Let me rephrase that and put it a little more bluntly: they're lies. Years ago, I struggled to sing a particular worship song that was melodically beautiful, but just not honest: 'Surely the presence of the Lord is in this place, I can feel God's mighty power and God's grace.'

Well, that's OK, I suppose – except that God is always around, whether I feel His mighty power or not. Sometimes I feel nothing, but that doesn't make Him any less real. I thought this Christian walk was more about faith than feelings... right? But it's the next part that nudges me to much gnashing of teeth, which isn't good for my soul, and not helpful for my dental arrangements either: 'I can hear the brush of angels' wings, I see glory on each face.'

I can't help but roll my eyes at the notion that I can look around at the average Sunday morning congregation and see glory on each face. Over there is young Sue, wrestling with her three small children – one of whom appears to be a reincarnation of the Gaderene demoniac in his prior-to-meeting-Jesus condition. Fred asked me to pray about his recurring problems with haemorrhoids last Sunday, and from the look on his face, he's having another flare-up. His painfully contorted facial features reveal discomfort about sitting on that hard wooden pew. They aren't a display of 'glory' because he's lost in wonder love and praise. And more seriously, there's grey-haired, utterly lovely Doris sitting in the pew behind me. She lost her Jim to pancreatic cancer just two months ago, and any type of music quickly reduces her to tears. She cries at toilet paper adverts on TV. Her faced is streaked now, but it's not because she's so thrilled that Jim is with Jesus (although she's grateful beyond words for that). The fact that he's there means that he's not here with her, which is where she'd rather have him be. If only Jim could have a day pass back to this side of death – just a few more hours spent holding hands, together once more. I see grief, not glory, on her face.

The song creates a portrait of the Church that just isn't accurate, and not just because of the diverse experiences of any congregation. Yes, Scripture chronicles those times when the clouds parted and the glory of God was revealed to humans, and while there was one occasion when a chap's face shone as a result (that would be Moses), the more usual human response doesn't tend to be quite so shiny. Gideon stammered and blustered because he was outright terrified. Elijah folded his arms, hunched down deeper in a dank cave, and repeated a prayer for death. Jonah ran, and then whined and bleated when he got a little sunburn. Presence doesn't always create glory.

But back to all that swooshing of angelic feathers. Here's the fact: when we declare that we can hear the brush of angels' wings, we lie.

Bluntly, we can't.

Some will argue that we're just declaring something metaphorically; poetically. But here's the nagging anxiety about all this that I just can't shake off. What about Dave, the 20-year-old sitting at the back of the congregation? Having put on weight recently because of the weekly consumption of Alpha-generated quiche, Dave has recently given his life to Jesus. He's keen, but somewhat confused, and his enthusiasm is making his confusion more acute. He really wants to serve Jesus, but is very much trying to figure what living a life of faith looks and feels like. And now Dave has a look on his face, and it's not glory. He's bewildered. Something of a literalist, he thinks that everyone else regularly bumps into angels (or at least hears them as they zip by). He doesn't have that experience, and wonders if he ever will. *Is there something wrong with me?* he asks, even as he tries to concentrate on singing the song.

There are other Christian 'truisms' that simply aren't true, like the bumper sticker that insensitively insists, 'If God seems far away, guess who's moved?' In other words, when we feel deserted, abandoned, unheard in our walk of faith (which is part of the deal – read the Psalms for confirmation), this must mean that we are deliberately placing a gap between us and God. Great, now I feel somewhat alone, and guilty with it, because *I've moved*. But sometimes God seems far away because life is tough, because our hormones are playing up, because we didn't sleep well last night, and sometimes... because He has apparently moved. The ancients called these seasons *Deus Absconditus* – the time when God seems to abscond. It appears that God will at times allow us to feel that He is not there, even though He has promised that He is.

There are plenty of other Christian slogans that set my teeth on edge and make my heart sink, but for now, let me just comment on one more, a slogan that often decorates Christian fridges and mantelpieces: 'If you want to hear God laugh, tell Him your plans.' I know that the general idea behind this saying is that God is far greater than us, knows everything that is knowable, and so for us to suggest any way forward is ridiculous in the extreme... except that, as I said earlier in this book, Jesus was and is open to suggestions about the miracles He performed. We then saw that extensive negotiations were held between God and Moses, prompting God to change His mind about the proposed plan to obliterate a city.

Not only that, but what kind of father would mock and jeer at the plans that His children present to Him? This notion of an aloof, sniffy, don't-you-dare-get-above-your-station-you-puny-humans kind of God is not the one I find in the Bible, or the one I've experienced in my Christian journey.

So just because Christians say it, doesn't make it true. And just because Christian leaders and preachers say it with authoritative voices and put it down on paper, doesn't make what they say true either. And that, of course, includes what I say and write...

I wish I'd known...
THAT SOME HEROES GO UNCELEBRATED

John Lennon sang the question: 'So this is Christmas, and what have you done?' Well, I'll tell you what many of us will do when Christmas comes around. We'll fret about getting a present for Dad (according to surveys, the most difficult family member to buy for). We'll vow to watch our weight over the Yuletide season, but then eat rather a lot – the average consumption is a whopping 7,000 calories on Christmas Day (a fact that creates great anxiety among the turkey population). We'll unpack those tree lights that didn't work last year, and will be disappointed to discover that they still don't work this year. We will hunt in vain for the single rogue dud bulb that is causing the whole string to stay dark. We'll pack them away, just so we can get irritated with them again next year. And then we'll frantically scribble our way through a stack of Christmas cards, sighing with relief when the job is done.

I'm not thrilled with the way some of those cards portray the holy family. And it's not just that they look mildly fluorescent, surreally glowing. Mary always looks beatific, and Jesus is either looking blissfully peaceful (because, as another song says, 'Little Lord Jesus, no crying He makes'), or He's sitting up already, chatting with the wise men. And the gathered bovine congregation of cows and donkeys are all grinning. But it's the absence of Joseph, a key player in the nativity drama, that bothers me – because he is usually nowhere to be seen. Maybe the absent carpenter is off fixing a wonky coffee table somewhere. Or perhaps his great contribution to the incarnation has just not been appreciated.

The stepfather of Jesus doesn't get huge profile. Mark's Gospel doesn't include him at all, and Matthew doesn't mention him after the second chapter. The Bible doesn't tell us how or when he died. But Joseph displayed some great character traits. Able to admit after his first angelically inspired dream that he had been wrong, he reversed his decision to break off his engagement to Mary. That alone makes him a great man in my book, because some people never quite come to the realisation that they are not always right. His decision to stand by Mary surely didn't come without a struggle: the law demanded that he report her as a suspected adulterer. He likely wrestled between a legal conscience and love. Thankfully, love won the day.

And then Joseph had the ability to be steered by the divine choreographer. Warned in another dream about Herod's impending infanticide campaign, he relocated the family to Egypt. A third dream revealed that it was finally safe to return to Israel. Yet another nocturnal message led him to actually settle the family in Nazareth.

Together with Mary, he was self-controlled too. Joseph marries Mary, and they enter into their marriage with all of the normal sexual anticipation that newlyweds feel. But there's no wedding night, no honeymoon for a while. Ensuring that the status of the virginal conception of Jesus is protected, Joseph and Mary wait until after He is born before beginning a normal married life together.

Following God is a wonderful privilege, but is sometimes extremely painful. Mary's life of suffering is well documented, but Joseph knew his fair share of struggles too. He trusted when, in the centre of God's will, he found that everything isn't plain sailing. The God who arranged a virgin birth didn't book them a room in Bethlehem.

Joseph didn't even get to choose the name of the child – that was determined by angelic revelation. And there were other pangs, and times of confusion, like when the boy Jesus went missing at the temple and then responded, without a hint of unkindness, 'I had to be in my Father's house.' Surely that was a moment of potential pain as Joseph was once again reminded – he was at best the stepfather to this most remarkable child, who was not his flesh and blood.

Joseph probably died before the public ministry of Jesus. He didn't get to witness the wondrous works of the lad he'd raised. Sometimes life is tough, but the call to stay faithful remains.

So Joseph lived beautifully – behind the scenes, often unapplauded. This Christmas, this Sunday, this year, there are most likely heroic souls who serve, trust, work, or give relentlessly, but who are also unsung heroes. Why not change that with a tender word of thanks? They might sense the encouragement of God through your smile, and find fresh strength in their serving, a great gift indeed.

And so this is Christmas, Joseph, and what have you done?

Quite a lot, I'd say.

I wish I'd known...
THAT GOD OFTEN DOES ODD STUFF

I'm biased, but I do think that we Brits produce some of the best television drama in the world. Bitterness nips me when, while out of the country, I try to log on to TV catch-up services online, only to be told that I'm not allowed. I pay my licence fee, so there should be a way, and I'm angry... Sorry, end of rant.

Anyway, Kay and I had watched a series all the way through in a mammoth binge-watching session, and had enjoyed it thoroughly. The series ended, and we heard that it was not going to be renewed. It's strange when you mourn the loss of entirely fictional characters that you've never met, but once we knew that our time with their story was ended, we felt irrationally sad.

Some weeks later, back in America, I had a dream about the series. It included the principal character and one of the supporting actresses. I dreamed that she had died (in real life), and that he was heartbroken at the loss. In my dream, he gave a press statement paying tribute to her fine acting skills and said that she would be greatly missed. I woke up in a sweat. The dream had been vivid. Eventually getting back to sleep, I immediately dreamed the same dream. I woke up again, and then went back to sleep, and the same thing happened. Wide awake now at 3am, I wondered – what was all this about?

Wandering into my office, I sat down at my computer, googled that lead actor's name, and pressed 'news'. And that's when everything got very strange indeed. An hour earlier, that actor had issued a press release about a colleague, saying how sad he was at the news of her passing. While I was dreaming that she died, she died. This was crazy. I sat staring at my computer screen for a very long time, wondering why on earth this had happened. I couldn't believe that this was just a random coincidence. God had something to do with this. But what, and why?

I did what I usually do when I'm bewildered (which is often): I prayed. And it was then that a wild thought landed in my mind, seemingly out of nowhere, which is usually how I hear from God.

'Make contact with that actor. And tell him that I love the people that he loves.'

What?

This was crazy. For one thing, I had no way of getting hold of this household name. And then the message that I was supposed to deliver was strange in itself – there was no overt mention of Jesus being the one who gives hope, no invitation to come to Christ, just this: 'God loves the people that you love.'

I turned to Facebook, and searched for the actor's 'fan' page, which can have unlimited subscribers. Unsurprisingly, he had millions – literally. There was no way I could make a meaningful connection through social media. I sat back in my chair, pondering. And then I remembered that a distant friend – one I had not seen for years – had some contact with this celebrity earlier in life, before he became famous. Perhaps he still had a connection.

I emailed him, and very quickly got a response. Not only were the two still connected, but they were getting together for a meal within a few days. This was getting very interesting indeed. With some hesitation, I emailed again, sharing the details of the dream, the timing of it, and the message that I felt was behind it. I added that I wasn't asking for any personal contact with the celebrity in question – in fact, I wasn't asking for anything, except for a message to be passed on. To my delight, my friend was willing to be the messenger.

A week went by. My email box chirped that I had a new message, and it was my distant friend. The two had got together. Details of the dream had been passed on. The actor's response had been a stunned silence, and he'd asked my friend to pass on his heartfelt thanks.

What has all this led to? I have no idea. But I do know that God does odd things at times. That's not a licence for craziness, but when we feel nudged by the Holy Spirit, and careful consideration suggests that we are on track with being a part of something that God is up to, we need to get with His programme.

And the identity of that by now world-famous celebrity? I promised back then that I would never reveal publicly who he is, and I intend to keep that pledge. Who knows? Perhaps God might trust me with another dream for someone else sometime.

As I end this book, and have reviewed some of the truths that I wish I'd known back when I began this Christian journey, I am grateful. I'm a stumbling soul, one who has had a spiritual stagger rather than a consistent walk. If I'm spared, 20 years from now I'll surely look back at the 61-year-old me, and rue the fact that there were still so many things I wish I'd known. The fresh-faced teenaged convert is no more, but the need to learn certainly remains.

These days, I have a life-purpose statement, a sentence that, for me, captures my reason for being alive. It's deeply personal, but allow me to share it with you:

'Eager to be a good man rather than just live the good life, I will learn, laugh, and experience and share the loving kindness of Jesus, especially in my family.'

I've crafted that sentence, because this I know for sure: God is love, God is good, and God is faithful. Peter, our water-walking hero, discovered that to be true. Shrugging off the temptation to be defined by his lowest moment and biggest failure, he rose to become the spokesperson at Pentecost and a dynamic catalyst in the fledgling Early Church. And his friends – who stayed in the boat – also discovered that same beauty of Jesus. Some say that when the Bible declares, 'Surely goodness and mercy follow me', the word used for 'follow' is a hunting term: goodness and mercy will *track me down*. I love that. The majority of the little gaggle of frightened disciples who stayed dry that day (well, as dry as is possible in the middle of a storm) found Christ's goodness to be good enough to live in, and good enough to die for.

During the four or so decades that God and I have been ambling along together, He has surprised me by being kinder than I ever imagined He could be. Wherever you are in the Christian trek, or if you are still considering beginning a journey with Jesus, may that be your discovery too.

The Cactus Stabbers	I Was Just Wandering…	It's a Dog's Life
ISBN: 978-1-78259-327-0	ISBN: 978-1-85345-850-7	ISBN: 978-1-78259-543-4

More from Jeff Lucas

Jeff takes a different view of some of his more peculiar moments – from causing mass road rage with his inability to change a tyre, to spending quality time with God at a rubbish dump. These books illustrate how God can redeem Jeff's mishaps and show him, and us, the brighter side of life.

e Also available in eBook format

As well as these, there is a whole range of books and DVDs by Jeff Lucas for you to explore at **www.cwr.org.uk/jefflucas**

Be inspired by God.
Every day.

Confidently face life's challenges by equipping yourself daily with God's Word. There is something for everyone...

Life Every Day
Jeff Lucas helps apply the Bible to daily life through his trademark humour and insight.

Every Day with Jesus
Selwyn Hughes' renowned writing is updated by Mick Brooks into these trusted and popular notes.

Inspiring Women Every Day
Encouragement, uplifting scriptures and insightful daily thoughts for women.

The Manual
Straight-talking guides to help men walk daily with God. Written by Carl Beech.

To find out more about all our daily Bible reading notes, or to take out a subscription, visit **www.cwr.org.uk/biblenotes** or call 01252 784700. Also available in Christian bookshops

 Printed format   Large print format   Email format   Ebook format

Discover more about CWR, our ministry, training and all our resources at www.cwr.org.uk